LIE-WARE

Reclaiming Truth in a Divided Nation

RALEIGH COFFIN

Lie-Ware

ISBN: 978-1-970153-59-0
Library of Congress Control Number: 2025926931

Disclaimer:
The content of this book represents the opinions, interpretations, and viewpoints of the author and is intended for informational and commentary purposes only. Certain statements may be based on personal belief, analysis, or speculation and are not intended to be presented as established or proven facts. Readers are encouraged to conduct their own research and form their own conclusions. The author disclaims any liability for errors, omissions, or interpretations contained herein.

Preamble to the Declaration of Independence
July 4, 1776

We hold these truths to be self-evident, that all men are created equal, that they are endowed by their Creator with certain unalienable Rights, that among these are Life, Liberty, and the pursuit of Happiness.

Introduction

Our country has been virtually split into two distinct mindsets, two parties, and two widely divergent views on how the country should be run.

I firmly believe in the two-party system, but I feel deep sorrow over the bifurcated situation today and the extent to which reporting has evolved into misinformation, Lawfare, hate, and conflict creation.

This split is not in the best interest of the United States or our country's future progress. And the hate will be growing until we are looking at either a drastic change in government, or a change of thought processes and attitudes toward civil disobedience. This division in America I lay firmly at the feet of both the left and right-wing Media. To understand this division, we need to examine a brief poll conducted for the Fourth of July weekend. This survey was conducted to determine how proud voters felt to be American.

Republicans	88%
Independents	55%
Democrats	35%

This is a shocking result, although for a long time, we've known the Democratic public feels victimized. Sure, they think that they have a tyrant as their President, and have no faith in recent actions and bills passed. They also were let down by the bending of the truth by their liberal media and their party, which have used many mistruths in their reporting. Many are unaware and still refuse to understand the LIE-WARE distortion.

Looking at ICE riots in Los Angeles, the "Kings Day" protests, the attempts to block the "Big Beautiful Bill," the two near assaults on Trump's life, and Schumer's leadership in the White House, I.C.E raid policies, and Charlie Kirk's slaughter. Between the government's closure in October 2025 and its two closures again in 2026, the unaddressed levels of crime suggest we may already be approaching a civil crisis.

The deep divide over how Americans now think and act is not good for our country. We should respect the First Amendment and people's rights to say what they think, but there should never be destruction of properties, broad-scale stealing, bombing buildings, civil distrust, hate mongering, and a complete misunderstanding of everything the other party is trying to do.

However, right now Democrats seem to prefer being more combative than discerning, more critical than supporting, more antagonistic than collaborative. For many years, left-wing media have had a monopoly on just about all news and have been associated with the shading of news, but as some of their coverage becomes increasingly preposterous and not in line with recent events or the truth, many citizens are moving more to conservative and independent reporting. But the fact remains, there are still over seventy million voters who look at the current presidency with disdain, hate, and uncertainty. Alongside this division, several sub-currents in public thought seem to coincide with intense human permissiveness and misguided thinking.

I hope this book will alert voters to the division in the country, which may already have had a disastrous impact on our democracy, and underscore the need for greater pragmatism and cooperation among our politicians. Democrats should prioritize voting on issues that benefit the American people rather than remain idle. The recent shutdown or Schumer's swansong is an example of policies that, in my view, have had negative impacts on the public.

As President Obama recently said to the Democratic Congress, "Show some spine."

How do we get here? How could two bodies of the United States be so diverse and antagonistic to each other? To understand all this, I think we need to examine a brief history of media and how today's media has become such a potent yet divisive force in politics.

Table of Contents

BOOK ONE

Chapter 1 | HISTORY OF MEDIA

"If it doesn't bleed, it won't lead!"
William Randolph Hearst.

Media bias has *increased* over time. In other words, bad news is more interesting than good news.

"To maintain objectivity in journalism, journalists should present the facts, whether they like or agree with them or not. Objective reporting is meant to report events in a neutral and unbiased manner, regardless of the writer's opinion or personal beliefs."
(Source: Wikipedia)

Although I never actually worked in a network newsroom, I did work simultaneously for both CBS and Fox; therefore, I had many occasions to see "the sausage being made."

The networks are only three blocks apart in New York City. My office was in what is now the News Corp (Fox) building, and the CBS building was just up the street.

I reported equally to both CBS and Fox. Raw news would usually come into the newsroom, be massaged, and then be rebranded as "now ready to broadcast," which meant it had been made "believably slanted." The degree of "slanting" in the 1980s and 1990s was tame and less pronounced than it is today. News items today are put through a "political strainer" in favor of the related party to influence voters.

CBS

At CBS in the 1960s, Walter Cronkite "read" the news with virtually no editorial interpretation.

This was a straightforward fifteen-minute newscast, but in 1963, with some network trepidation, it was increased to thirty minutes.

At the time, CBS management questioned whether the public had an interest in a full half-hour of news; however, they persisted and ultimately achieved success. Cronkite "read" the news, and then the viewer moved to "I Love Lucy," presumably relieved to be watching something entertaining.

You should also be aware that the news operations were "loss leaders" at all three networks (CBS, NBC, ABC), but network management stuck with news events almost as a Public Service Announcement (PSA).

When Cronkite retired from CBS News, he retained a seat on the board, and the network went on to feature Dan Rather for the next twenty-four years. Dan introduced considerable slanting, although not to the same degree as today. We once asked Dan where he figured CBS was on the political spectrum. He declared "middle of the road."

I thought at the time that if CBS was middle of the road, he must have meant the "middle of the far-left lane."

CBS was also, in part, dependent on news services like AP, which provided mostly left-wing messaging.

In the 1990s, with extensive slanting, targeted advertising, and network management, advertisers were delighted to see the New News gradually become profitable.

Besides explaining how the viewer should think about the news, several other factors contributed to this *New News.*

In the 1980s, CNN founder Ted Turner surprised the world by broadcasting twenty-four hours a day, seven days a week, which also meant 24/7 advertising sales. The networks received a significant boost in 1991 when viewers, in a state of patriotic fervor, closely followed coverage of the Gulf War. CNN provided outstanding coverage, including footage of actual Gulf War battles, Washington, D.C.'s involvement, military interviews, and other key moments. Its audience grew.

This, of course, was duly noted by the three established networks, CBS, NBC, and ABC, and it followed that the major networks could move newsrooms from loss leaders to profit producers, not only by becoming more sensational but also by expanding round-the-clock coverage. The news division eventually became a bright diamond for the Tiffany network (CBS) as it moved from raw, mostly unadulterated news in the days of Walter Cronkite to a more edgy 'interpretation' of the news with 24/7 exposure, more sensationalism, stretching of the truth, and increased use of LIE-WARE over time, becoming an increasingly important Bully Pulpit for the Democratic Party.

How did the party affiliations become such a factor in handling the established networks' news events?

I examined the historical reasoning behind the tremendous prominence and monopoly of left-wing news, which, I believe, controlled approximately 90% of total news in the U.S. for several decades.

Cronkite/Vietnam

Until 1968, Cronkite continued to "read" the news, generally supporting Lyndon Johnson's early claims that the U.S. was winning the war.

Later that year, Cronkite went to Vietnam just after the disastrous TET offensive and assessed that, at best, it would be a draw, with the U.S. not succeeding.

He publicly announced his skepticism nationwide regarding President Johnson's claims that the United States would prevail.

Johnson said, "If I've lost Cronkite, I've lost the country." And indeed he did, as LBJ chose not to run for another term. This was a clear example of how the media's power could be used for good, changing the minds of millions.

As other media outlets observed this power, they increased their efforts to try to change men's minds by shaping the news.

For the first time, Cronkite took a strong position on what appeared to be a deadlock, marked by heavy losses of men and material.

Initially, Americans had been fairly positive and aggressive about the war and the confrontation with communism in the Far East, but after several months, the war's toll in lives began to take its toll. Cronkite brought this to the fore upon his return from the Tet Offensive, when he broadcast his skepticism about the Vietnam War.

"To say that we are closer to victory today is to believe, in the face of evidence, the optimists who have been wrong in the past. To suggest we are on the edge of defeat is to yield to unreasonable pessimism. To say that we are mired in stalemate seems the only realistic, yet unsatisfactory, conclusion. . . . But it is increasingly clear to this reporter that the only rational way out then will be to negotiate, not as victors, but as an honorable people who lived up to their pledge to defend democracy, and did the best they could."

–Walter Cronkite

Bill Paley/Harry K. Smith/Dan Rather

Bill Paley, founder and chairman of CBS, did as much as possible to ensure that reporting remained true to the facts. He approved of Cronkite but fired Howard K. Smith for "invention." Smith's contract prohibited editorializing, and his article on Birmingham had prompted a lawsuit against CBS.

Paley also had frequent problems with Dan Rather for cooking the facts, but never so egregious as to eliminate Rather.

Years later, Rather was fired for questioning George W. Bush's educational and military credentials.

In my view, Paley was the last bulwark of Truth in Media. His death in 1990 enabled a new hands-off approach, with reporting rules broadly expanded, seemingly to foster interpretive reporting and ultimately LieWare.

FOX

In 1986, a new power emerged. Rupert Murdoch, an Australian business mogul and newspaper magnate, had just acquired 20th Century Fox.

Early in his ownership of Fox, Rupert came to see me and my division, later known as Fox Home Entertainment, at our New York City office, which is now the News Corp building and is frequently referred to as the "Fox Building" on Sixth Avenue.

Today, the building also houses other Murdoch-owned properties, including the Wall Street Journal, Barron's, the New York Post, and the Fox Network, which includes Fox News and Fox Business.

Rupert explained that he planned to create the FOX Television Network to compete with CBS, ABC, and NBC. Frankly, most of us had to hold our tongues on this one, as it seemed like a crazy concept and an overreach to me and many in the network business, who felt there was no room for a fourth network and that the huge expense of almost three billion dollars (not including large subsequent content deals) would be wasted. Additionally, Rupert's strong conservatism and the network's likely lean made less sense given that American viewers expected "democratized" news stories.

In 1986, decades after the three major networks had launched, Rupert introduced a conservative Fox network that would also emulate them, offering serials, adventure films, sports, romances, comedies, news, and special events.

At first, it was hard for Rupert and Fox's new hire, Barry Diller, to secure talent. Hollywood stars and directors resisted the idea of a conservative network, fearing marginalization and the loss of future opportunities to the left-wing controllers of both Networks and Hollywood Studios. The going was slow. The first efforts, The Tracey Ullman Show and the Joan Rivers Show, drew anemic ratings.

However, Fox News was gaining traction among more conservative viewers, who welcomed a counterbalance to the left-leaning mindset of the existing networks. Fox News led the rest of the network into profitability, and today, in 2025, it is the most-watched broadcast and cable news network.

Fox played a major role in reinstating Donald Trump as the President of the United States, following a dismal four-year performance by Biden, the White House, and allied left-wing politicians. But the country remains sharply divided, and Democratic voters were largely shut out of the truth by the partisan spin of their own media. For example, Biden's mental and physical state was concealed, along with any meaningful achievements during what I believe were the most destructive four years of any U.S. presidency.

In recent months, others have come to agree with this assessment, and many liberals now admit that false information from the White House completely blindsided them. They had been pushing their president's agenda and even assuring viewers that Kamala would win the 2024 election.

As the truth became clearer, they threw their hands up in dismay.

Fox News was not consistent in reporting the truth 100% of the time, but at the turn of the twenty-first century, it did not have the same clout and mass media effect on viewers that it does today. A new definition: A good newsman researches stories first for facts, then may add some sensationalism or interpretation to appeal to their viewers, who are typically affiliated with a particular party. All networks did this to varying degrees.

Roger Ayles

In 1996, Roger Ayles took over as CEO and chairman of Fox News. He was a showman, a leader, and, to many, a womanizer. He built Fox News by bringing attractive newspeople, entertainment, and sex to the network, boosting ratings. He insisted on glass tables for the female masters of ceremonies to show off their legs and hired the most beautiful women.

After twenty years of success, Ayles was fired by Murdoch due to Ayles' own casting couch, which was used to exert heavy pressure on young, beautiful aspirants.

Finally, his habits reached the press through an outspoken Gretchen Carlson, who made no bones about his advances. Gretchen was a former Miss America who had repelled Roger's advances and then sued him for them. Megyn Kelly also rebuffed Ayles' advances and waged her own private battle with him and Donald Trump. As a result, Megyn and several other headliners, including Bill O'Reilly and Andrea

Tantaros, were let go by Ayles. Then he was fired by Rupert himself. His severance was $40 million, while Kelly and Gretchen each received $20 million.

The Roger Ayles interlude spanned twenty years, from 1996 to 2016. Ayles was quite a showman. He recognized talent and understood how political contention and sex appeal shaped audience appreciation. Today, the "Five" (created by Roger Ayles) is the highest-rated TV news show in the U.S. The four Republicans versus one Democrat, the contention it raises, and the astuteness of its panelists draw viewers.

The 2019 movie "BOMBSHELL" did a good job of covering Gretchen and Megyn's story, as well as Roger's personality. Featuring Nicole Kidman, Margo Robbie, and Charlize Theron added to the film and justified the title "Bombshell."

Streaming

Streaming is aimed at the growing audience that has left or cut away from broadcast, but still wants some of these services. Over the last three years, there has been a significant shift from traditional broadcast to these streaming combinations.

At our first NYC meeting, Rupert showed a keen interest in all aspects of the entertainment and broadcasting industries. We tried to answer all his far-ranging questions. He rightly felt there was huge potential for home entertainment via streaming in the near future, which, of course, was music to my ears. We did not yet have the term "Streaming" in our lexicon, but we were pushing toward the ability to see any movie, watch any sitcom, or play any game electronically, all from the comfort of your home. No going to the video store, no receiving videos sent by Cash on Delivery, no lock-ins for timing. For the most part, we all felt this was the ultimate in entertainment and would revolutionize how people saw television and cable specials, learned, zoomed, and communicated while relaxing in their own homes.

How did party affiliations become such a factor in how the established networks handled news events? Why were the studios and networks so left-wing in the first place?

I looked at the historical reasoning behind the left-wing news media's tremendous prominence and monopoly.

Chapter 2 | Origin of Entertainment

Give me your tired and your poor.
Your Masses yearning to be free."

(This phrase appears on the Statue of Liberty and was written by Emma Lazarus.)

Many years ago, in the 1980s and 1990s, while I was working on the film side at CBS and Fox, I read Neal Gabler's book, "An Empire of Their Own: How the Jews Invented Hollywood."

You must remember that in the early 20th century, immigrant Jews were generally barred from executive positions at corporations and were also denied entry to the "white shoe" law firms, banks, and established investment companies.

During that period, many of the immigrating Jews came from Germany and Eastern Europe, where they had been subjected to intense pogroms, prejudice, incarceration, firing squads, violence, virulent hate, and scorn. Because many of the immigrants were well-educated, they scanned the horizon for a place where they could fit in their new country: the U.S.A.

Eureka!

Nickelodeon silent movies were beginning to impact the U.S. population, and these potential Hollywood executives saw "the future of entertainment" as a huge new field not off limits to Jews. These enterprising new Jewish Americans started most of the major film businesses, including MGM, Fox, Columbia, Warner Bros., Universal, and Paramount.

Without any collusion or really any forethought, these clever Eastern Europeans, having escaped from tyranny and government abuses, initially leaned conservative but soon moved toward the Democratic Party as the party for the underdog.

When hiring executives, directors, actors, and others, they also sought individuals with similar backgrounds and worldviews.

Meanwhile, on the East Coast, the situation was not too different, as the concept of a broadcast network began to emerge. The major networks were also started by Jews, again mainly from Germany and Eastern Europe, who found the doors of commerce, industry, banking, and law firms in the U.S. slammed shut. So, onto the scene came the founders and officers of the networks, as inspired and developed by such greats as:

- **General David Sarnoff (NBC)**
- **William Paley (CBS)**
- **Leonard Goldenson (ABC)**

Not surprisingly, today, nearly all the original film studios predominantly vote liberal and have a relationship with the major liberal networks, first with Paramount, and CBS, then RCA, which was owned by NBC and has largely disappeared, leaving the NBC network to affiliate first with GE, then with Comcast, now the owners of NBC Universal.

The newsmen hired by these men leaned liberal and were convinced that the Democratic Party had the answers and was the main guiding force for our "tired and poor."

At the time, they were probably right!

The left formed unions, challenged child labor laws, supported women's suffrage, and promoted the "rights of the common man." They also championed landmark legislation that benefited all Americans, including bills such as:

- **G.I. Bill.**
- **Social Security**
- **Medicare**
- **Medicaid**

These Broadcast Giants and the executives they hired were in lockstep with the position that they were truly serving the country.

Chapter 3 | Major Policy Setbacks

"Democracy's a very fragile thing. You have to take care of it. As soon as you stop being responsible for it and allow it to become a scare tactic, it's no longer democracy, is it? It's something else. It may be an inch away from totalitarianism."

--Sam Shepard

Setback I - Immigration

Undocumented Aliens

Obviously, illegal immigrants who have already broken the law upon entering the U.S. should be expelled immediately if they are identified as undocumented and/or caught committing crimes against Americans. To keep the courts out of it, there should ideally be a sentence with an automatic verdict, accompanied by immediate "repatriation," to avoid a lengthy court procedure. This may be ideal, but it is not practical. The insistence by the Democrats that every undocumented immigrant should go to trial is totally unrealistic. This would take over twenty years and would be difficult to locate the embedded alien after a couple of years; the effort would probably achieve nothing. I'm afraid this is another Law-Fare effort by liberals to impede the cleansing of our country from the negative impact of open borders.

The Trump White House, offering to pay a $1,000 - $3,000 premium to leave plus a free air ticket, will help, but it will only be taken up by a segment of the illegal immigration population. I would guess that twenty percent would be happy with this, even if it is a low estimate. This is an efficient policy that not only provides a good solution to the problem of illegal activity but also saves taxpayers' time and money.

Millions of immigrants crossing the border unlawfully each year will take a negative toll on our treasury, our lifestyle, our children, and our crime rate, particularly if undocumented immigrants are not expelled.

The media, the politicians, the financial establishment, and even some of our opinion writers have not recognized or evaluated the true impact on our economy of up to twenty million illegal immigrants admitted into this country through 2025.

One arbitrary way to break it down is as follows:

Total Illegals (Estimate)	20.0 M
Having full-time jobs	6.0 M
Part-time jobs	3.5 M
Family ties	2.0 M
Independent means	1.0 M
Unemployed	2.0 M
Criminals (known)	1.5 M
Desperate	4.0 M
Total	20.0 Million

Amid all the pre-election crossfire between the two parties, I believe a major element of what the Biden-Harris White House has done to this country has not yet been fully evaluated. Consider the impact of the open-border situation, which has allowed illegal aliens to enter and measurably reduced our standard of living now and in the future. Finally, it appears that some Democrats are starting to believe the responsible press and to disbelieve established media institutions that, in my view, often align closely with and amplify the Biden administration's messaging.

The Biden White House claims it didn't know about his incompetence and memory problems, and that Dr. O'Connor never indicated or reported that any memory test was performed on the president. The prostate screening, using standard PSA tests for all men over fifty, was conducted.

The latest estimate I have heard for the cost of supporting undocumented immigrants is a bill of $200 billion per year. I think this is orders of magnitude too low, and we are already in a position where the standard of living in our country will have to be reduced because the need for additional services will have to be greatly increased. For example:

I believe the following will need to be increased by two to three times the current annual expense just to service the inflow, even if we are aggressive about the removal policy.

Before any direct financial support to the illegals by the U.S. government, I see a strong need to expand:

- Prisons/Guards
- Police Stations
- Border Control
- Ice
- Transportation
- Medical Services
- Medical Offices
- Hospital Workers
- Street Sanitation
- Schools And Teachers

- Affordable Housing
- Legal Representation

The above, which I think will cost our economy at least $1 trillion a year now, is growing exponentially.

By my own estimates, I see approximately four to six million immigrants (see above) in desperate circumstances, which will unfortunately increase the crime rate, as their eventual need to steal food from stores, catch whatever wildlife they can, including domestic pets, and invade and forcibly take over our homes, which they have already begun to do.

This will cost our country trillions until the situation is addressed and a sound immigration policy is in place. We are trying to send them back, but the Democrats have hyped this as an inhuman and immoral act and want to cling to these potential future Democratic voters. Plus, Democratic cities, especially Minneapolis, and other states have fought against ICE and its efforts to round up illegals.

The recent "Big Beautiful Bill" once again highlights the Democrats' desire to impede progress and the benefits to U.S. citizens. Using data from the CBO, which does not dynamically score, hinders what we can do now to fix our problems because the CBO relies primarily on lagging or past indicators.

Democratic leaders often criticize these policies, though I believe some of the broader impacts are underappreciated.

Looking at the big picture as it stands in 2025, I believe there should be serious investigations into who really controlled Biden during his four years in office and into the use of his autopen.

So-called experts have said that the liberal Democratic Party oversaw the Biden administration.

The fact that most of Biden's actions were not halted but put into force was so parallel to those I think of as "the Chinese objectives for weakening the United States."

This should concern every citizen, every lawmaker, every cabinet member, the two major parties, and the White House. It has been called the worst scandal in United States history. We must look beyond a cadre of 'libs' and advisers who were in the White House at the time. Congress should undertake a thorough investigation, possibly with the assistance of a Blue-Ribbon Special Counsel comprising doctors, lawyers, or executives with management experience and profit responsibility. If we can pinpoint those involved in Biden's policy decisions, I believe they have caused harmful consequences. In my view, many of the Biden administration's policies have had significant negative effects. They have advanced policies that some critics argue may have inadvertently benefited geopolitical competitors such as Russia and China.

Regarding Biden's Health Record, as stated, something should be instituted, such as a Medical Committee that annually reviews the president's condition, both mental and physical. There are now tests that take ten minutes or less, such as the Montreal Cognitive Assessment, which can identify mental health issues (and point to further diagnosis and testing). They need not necessarily report the annual results to the public unless they discover the possibility of an unfit leader.

An important part of this allegedly extensive health review would be to examine why Biden did not have his PSA tested for four years while president. This is highly unlikely, and it is possible that these tests were conducted but never disclosed to the American public.

The White House, which held back recognition of his mental acuity, appears to have also ignored the president's stage-four prostate cancer, so it could hardly be a recent event.

Again, I am concerned that there may have been a lack of full transparency and control. Similarly, I see a need for an investigation into the previous president's mental acuity and into how his decline was never reported to the left-wing press or any press, nor "discovered" by the White House. We are now hearing stories, sadly, that the country was dealing with a man with prostate cancer and mental problems who was kept from press conferences, meetings with Congress, and meetings with his Cabinet, and who appeared in public only for structured press statements.

Could Dr. Jill Biden and the "Politburo" have overlooked these in his physical tests, or did they deliberately ignore and suppress any abnormalities in his PSA or mental scores? Or were they never reported by Dr. O'Connor?

As it stands, we're having a problem digging out from the damage done, but as I've explained above, I think the impact of the twenty-odd million illegal immigrants will be a lasting, major cost for the years ahead and, if not confronted, could actually lead us into third-world status or at least civil disobedience.

Biden's open-borders plan has inflicted a costly social and financial blow that could last for the next decade and, if not resolved, may reduce our country to a third-rate republic.

Democrats seem determined to prevent the repatriation of illegal immigrants and to thwart every Republican attempt to address what I see as a deeply harmful and growing national problem.

Due Process and Lawfare

There is a difference in the due process afforded to non-Americans and to our citizens. Americans who have committed a felony, for example, are subject to a thorough legal process that involves lawyers, a judge, and, in some cases, a jury.

When an alien is caught crossing our border, their due process is generally limited to a statement of the law they have violated and signing a form, after which they are immediately returned across the border (or, if necessary, to their country of origin). There will hopefully be exceptions for Dreamers, i.e., those who entered the country as babies or children and have since integrated. The Democrats have demanded due-process protections for all twenty million entrants, which AI said is totally unworkable.

Setback II - Politburo/Autopen

I've read many reports, without pointing fingers, that raise serious concerns about the Biden presidency in our country's history. Clearly, the right-wing press raised questions about Biden's medical acuity far earlier than his own party. The right-wing media also had the advantage of being correct on many aspects of the news for more than a year, including Hunter Biden's laptop, the Russian conspiracy, and the outlook for the 2024 election. In other words, they have been more truthful and factual, not just because the news has been favorable to them so far.

How did all this happen? Some commentators have even raised questions – without conclusive evidence – about whether foreign influence may have played a role in decision-making.

Actually, there are at least four autopens, intended primarily for ceremonial signing, but they were also considered valid as representing the president's agreement to a bill if he signed or authorized it.

As an old news junkie, I, of course, follow the fates of both parties and have watched with dismay as the Democratic narrative has become increasingly distorted, especially over the last ten years, as the mainstream media have led their voters and, apparently, themselves into a deep dive into despair and hatred.

Setback III - Energy

On the first day in office, Biden cut America's energy production by thirty percent by eliminating fracking, well drilling, and exploration. This move shifted us from a net energy exporter to a net importer of foreign oil.

Additionally, the U.S. was effectively cut off from exporting energy to NATO, India, and other friendly countries. This shifted their energy dependence toward our enemies, primarily Russia.

Lost is the wealth of our country's primary resources, which were reduced and, in many cases, mothballed.

As stated, Biden presided over the most destructive four years of any U.S. president's tenure. In recent months, others have come to agree with this assessment, and liberals are now explaining how they were misinformed by the White House. They had been relentlessly pushing their president's agenda and had almost promised their viewers that Kamala would win the election in '24. Then they threw their hands up in dismay at the loss.

The mainstream media, although they have been equally wrong, have probably been subverting our country and its interests for over twenty years and may not change. They will continue to be the hard-nosed group that lies, distorts facts, and promotes falsehoods, as they have been.

As one writer has put it, "the press hates Trump more than it loves the truth." (Michael Goodwin, New York Post.)

However, there could be a shift in voters' thinking. "How could the USA, the most admired, strongest, and most powerful country in the world, be ruled unconstitutionally by a small group of unelected officials, the 'Politburo'?" (see page 14)

I have previously argued that we appoint at least a Special Counsel to conduct an in-depth investigation into what happened, rather than merely wag our finger and say "I told you so" to the Democrats. First, we must determine how the Politburo was formed and under whose authority. We must also understand whether decision-making may have been concentrated among a small group whose priorities, critics argue, did not always align with broader U.S. interests.

And Dr. Jill Biden should not be blameless in this debacle. First, she insisted on being called Dr. Biden to enhance her position. She does have a doctorate in education, but that does not qualify her to be a caregiver for the allegedly most powerful man in the world. She seemed to urge him toward what the Politburo wanted, and she may have, perhaps unwittingly, used the powerful autopen to change policies and approve destructive actions. What was she thinking during their four disastrous years?

Biden is many things, but he has never been the brightest bulb in the box, and he will bend the truth if it makes his comments more concrete or his jokes funnier. He frequently takes the wrong action or makes the wrong decision, yet he has served his government for over 50 years. Before this debacle, we, the people, had never thought of him as a communist or even disloyal to this country. It is hard to believe that he knowingly signed each bill and the White House directives, yet he seemed to be a 'cat's paw' for possible members of the Politburo or those who called the shots. To whom did they report?

Interviews with government officials could protect us from future government infiltration. But in this case, they weren't 'Watching the Store.' The total harm done to our country by the Biden presidency, both today and in the future, remains unmeasured and may last for years, if not decades. It should never happen again, with better safeguards and oversight. The 25th Amendment is not enough if the White House is hiding a president's mental and physical problems.

Tapper

Jake Tapper, CNN News's head Washington anchor, is one of the many apologists whose book, Original Sin, explains how he was caught with his pants down. He claims he has a nose for news, yet failed to present an accurate picture of the president's health despite abundant evidence of the president's decline. Until the presidential debate, Tapper didn't see any problem with Biden's mental acuity and never questioned it, at least not publicly. On the contrary, he frequently proclaimed that the president was sharp and denied rumors of Biden's mental decline. But the Republicans saw the signs and tried to report them despite the mainstream media's loud and assertive cries of "FAKE NEWS."

As early as 2019, FOX News reported questions about Biden's capabilities. Again and again, viewers were informed that Joe Biden could not continue serving as president. We were supposed to believe Biden's falls and his blackouts signified nothing, just one-offs, while the left insisted Republicans were exaggerating Biden's repeated lapses and physical difficulties. Despite quoting scores of isolated reports in his book that suggested Biden's faulty mental acuity, Tapper had previously slammed Republicans' inferences. He and other members of the far left failed or chose not to acknowledge, much less report, that the president was not running on all cylinders—that is, until the presidential debate, when Democrats recoiled as they could no longer cover for Joe.

Now Tapper is making big bucks reporting on his so-called "ignorance." And in my opinion, at the same time, the book probably saved his job with CNN for a year or two as the public began to see through left-wing media deceptions.

This is the most scandalous event in the last 250 years. This far-left media block could have potentially brought down this country, as they watched but chose not to report truthfully.

Finally, everyone began to catch on, and by the first quarter of 2025, it was labeled "the most unprincipled acts of tyranny" ever recorded.

Tapper's Original Sin

Some view this book as humorous. I found the book to be a harbinger of tragedy for our country. Tapper now cites hundreds of indications of Biden's incompetence dating back to early 2017.

One example after another, all undetected by such experienced news hounds as Jake Tapper, was presented through these lies. Jake said he never considered the extent of the president's mental acuity problem. The book also illustrates the danger of LIE-WARE when a party lies to itself and its voters.

The Politburo Composition

Jeff Zients, White House Chief of Staff
Ron Klain, Former White House Chief of Staff

Mike Donilon, Senior Adviser/Chief Strategist to Biden
Anita Dunn, Senior Adviser to Biden
Steve Ricchetti, Counselor to Biden
Annie Tomasini, Director of Oval Office Operations

Biden Tapes

On October 8-9, 2023, Robert Hur recorded two 3-hour sessions of his conversations with Biden. If released at the time, these tapes would have quickly brought Biden's cognitive problems to the fore. Instead, the Biden team asserted "executive privilege," and the tapes were held for over a year before being released, along with the video, on March 12, 2024.

If the tapes had been audited by the Democratic Party and/or the reelection committee, they could have quickly uncovered the reason for Biden's hesitancy and provided the party with a rationale for not nominating Biden for a second try at the presidency. Instead, according to Tapper, because the tapes were not available until March 2024, the party did not have that option. Looking back, I feel there was still time to restructure the Democratic Party's presidential ticket. But the urgency did not surface until the debate.

Tapper's view was that if this information, along with numerous other ignored warnings about Biden's problems, had given them time to hold a 'runoff' between strong candidates and select a younger, sane prospect, it would have resulted in a much stronger

Democratic ticket. Instead, Kamala's nomination was a last resort, and this giddy, word-salad-speaking woman went down to a fairly large defeat on election day, in my opinion, saving the country from the continuation of Biden's errant policies of open borders, no tax relief, and reduced fossil energy in favor of 'green energy' that they promoted despite its reliance on large amounts of fossil fuels to implement.

Chapter 4 | DONALD J. TRUMP

2024 Presidential Election Debate

In this debate, Trump did not comport himself well, let alone favorably. Part of the blame lies with the commentators, who kept switching subjects from hot-button issues like the economy to abortion, one of the few subjects where Kamala could speak with confidence or had a clear opinion.

Trump ungraciously claimed that Democrats wanted to abort children even after birth. (post-birth abortion).

"If Democrats didn't already know the progressive agenda was a political loser (and Kamala Harris's campaign subterfuge proves they did), they do now. What to do with an ash heap of a political platform, one nonetheless rigidly enforced by liberal shock troops, and no charismatic figure with the spine or know-how to lead a change of direction? Engage muscle memory and do the easy first. Fight, fight, fight. Thus, the bizarre sight of Democrats rallying

fervently in favor of more government waste, fraud, and inefficiency. Expect this to continue."

--Kim Strassel
Wall Street Journal

Trump's debate style that evening was gratuitous and unnecessary, as his opponent Harris really did not have opinions on the border (except "keep it open"), how to solve our financial problems, or how to deal with our wars in the Middle East and Ukraine. Trump tried to overwhelm her rather than expose her ignorance. I was interested to see that an independent source that rates the veracity of each candidate's statements found only one lie in Kamala's statements and many egregious lies in Trump's. It is hard for me to credit the authenticity of this supposedly "objective" truth meter.

"You've got to admit that each party is worse than the other. The one that's out always looks best."

--Will Rogers

Trump's First-Term Accomplishments.

Before we discuss the man himself, I think it would be a good reminder to review his first term in office. During his first term, Donald Trump's administration pursued a variety of policy initiatives and achieved several notable outcomes. The following is a summary of key accomplishments.

1. Tax Cuts And Jobs Act (2017).

This legislation significantly reduced corporate and individual income tax rates, representing the largest tax overhaul since the 1980s. Now continued in the Big Beautiful Bill.

2. Deregulation
   The Trump administration implemented a broad deregulatory agenda to reduce regulatory burdens on businesses and startups. This has to be readdressed after Biden's term.

3. Trade Policy: Trump pursued an "America-First" trade policy, including renegotiating the North American Free Trade Agreement (NAFTA) into the United States-Mexico-Canada agreement. (USMCA)

4. Economic Growth
   The economy experienced sustained growth and a low unemployment rate during the early part of his term, until the COVID-19 pandemic triggered a significant economic downturn.

5. Judicial Appointments - Federal judges
   Trump appointed a large number of conservative judges to the federal courts, including three Supreme Court justices – Gorsuch, Kavanaugh, and Coney Barrett – shaping the judiciary in ways that continue to have a lasting impact.

6. National Security and Foreign Policy

The Trump administration oversaw the territorial defeat of the Islamic State (ISIS) in Iraq and Syria.

7. Military Spending
   Increased military spending and investment in U.S. defense capabilities. Now about $900 Billion.

8. Withdrawal From Agreements
   Trump withdrew the US from several international agreements and organizations, including the Paris Agreement on climate change and the Iran nuclear deal. These have obviously been carried over to his present term.

9. Space Force
   Established the Space Force as a new branch of the US military.

10. Criminal Justice Reform
    The First Step Act, a bipartisan bill, was signed into law and reformed federal prison and sentencing policies.
11. Energy Independence
    The U.S. briefly became a net exporter of natural gas for the first time since 1957, a position Biden reversed on his first day in office.

12. Right to Try Legislation

Signed legislation, granting terminally ill patients greater access to experimental treatments.

13. Opioid Epidemic Funding
    Secured funding to combat the opioid crisis.

14. Veterans Affairs Reforms
    Implemented reforms to improve services and accountability at the Department of Veterans Affairs.

Please note that these accomplishments are drawn from a variety of sources, including White House archives, The Week, and Wikipedia, and are based on an AI-generated overview. Some of the activities and accomplishments were affected by the COVID-19 outbreak.

When Trump received the Man of the Year award in 2024, I kept wondering whether China didn't also have a 'Man of the Year' award for good old Joe. He surely deserved it, as his administration did more than anyone to move China ahead of us in every possible way. As I said, he opened our borders to a crippling extent, cut our energy production by 30% on his first day in office, and has spent, baby, spent!

The Man

On the one hand, Trump has truly been a playboy/billionaire, full of pride and ego. Most likely a former womanizer (men—wouldn't some of you be if you were a young man with billions?). He is somewhat imprecise in his public statements. His grammar is not always correct, as evidenced by his frequent use of double negatives (e.g., They shouldn't never have done that). And sometimes he can be short on grace and even rude toward the opposition, as well as bombastic about his claims.

However, he is also a decisive businessman with clear strategic thinking on many of the issues we face daily. As noted, during his first presidential term, he demonstrated pragmatic leadership by raising family incomes, creating jobs across all classes, controlling inflation, expanding energy production, and reducing harmful regulations.

He's got three more years now, and in his remaining term, he can be just the ticket for what America needs after its four very expensive years under Biden, an administration that seemed determined to undermine our democracy by pushing many inappropriate policies, none more costly than open borders.

Trump appears to have a far-reaching vision and can undertake numerous large-scale projects simultaneously, delegating to and pushing for hand-selected individuals who will embrace and foster his ambitious objectives for the country.

He is a unique and unlikely candidate for President, but he may be the best we have ever had. He appears to possess exceptional administrative control and power, as well as the ability to juggle multiple tasks and successfully meet most challenges.

Using my own hyperbole, I see him as a God-given gift to a country that was about to be plunged further into debt and possibly ruin, a nation where life as we know it could vanish because of the last administration's unreasonable steps to allow millions of undocumented immigrants to enter the country unlawfully and to curtail all aspects of our energy, including fracking, Liquid Natural Gas, pipelines, and ANWAR exploration, at a time when Petrodollars pretty much rule the world and lead diplomacy. Iran has been temporarily defanged, but China is now its most significant and enduring problem.

I am sure that Trump has spent many sleepless hours thinking about China and how to respond. The Chinese Communist Party (CCP) has complete control of its nation and tells its largely automaton people what to do, when to do it, and how to do it. It also, of course, wants the entire world to be subordinate to its precepts.

Additionally, he acknowledges that China is preparing to confront the United States on every aspect and level of our lives, and may already be engaged in that fight.

The following section illustrates the extent and far-reaching nature of their plans to control the future.

To recap, what President Trump has done and is trying to do includes the following:

- Restoring energy independence.
- Drill, Baby, Drill!
- Paying down the national debt.
- Using strategic tariffs to bring international trade policies into balance.
- Eliminating tremendous waste in government

- Finding an economic and humane way to return illegal immigrants to their birth country or elsewhere.
- Supporting talented Americans across the nation so they can step in and contribute productively.
- Not necessarily keeping the GOP in permanent power, but helping to 'enlighten the Democrats' so they can have productive, fulfilling, and patriotic presidential terms of their own.
- Ensuring we never slide back to the Biden years, which, however unintentionally, inflicted so much damage on the United States.

Democrats want to stop a man like Trump, who is attempting the following:

Reduce Taxes
Regulation redirection
Balance Trade through judicious tariffs
Use Doge (to help eliminate Gov't waste") PLUS
Bring peace to Israel, Hamas, and the Palestinians

Efforts To
Eliminate Iran's nuclear capability
Stop the Ukraine War
Close the border
Balance the Fiscal Budget
Eliminate Waste and Fraud
Eliminate Gov't redundancy
Improve the U.S. world standing
Restore energy independence
Reduce LIE-WARE in all media.
Rein in China and push rare earth development

Eliminate Crime in many blue cities

It's hard for me to believe that any group as large as the Democratic Party would prevent the Trump Administration from achieving some or all of the above. But the Democrats are confronting the above with warped logic and innuendo, spurred on by the so-called elite media.

Democrats' View of the DJT

Of course, many hundreds of thousands, if not millions, were susceptible to the New York Times campaign for the last twenty years against this Trump 'ogre,' this hater of women, this playboy, this billionaire who is going to lead us into totalitarian disaster if he runs and wins his second term for another four years (Irrespective of a third term he has mentioned.) The answer, in my opinion, is that LIE-WARE created this. With the constant pounding by the mainstream media and press, the democrats have distorted the presidential term, which the faithful believe is the best in history. They failed when they picked apart a few of Trump's weaknesses, but created others based on pure theory and conjecture, and hyped them. It was a terrible picture of the world that the liberal press created, with very few of their viewers aware of reality, continuing to make them depressed and hateful.

But they did! And this seemed to foster the Trump Derangement Syndrome and hate, especially among housewives' image of Trump as an evil man who hated women and was truly a Nazi, who wants to eliminate the Department of Education, and ruin our country.

For many years, I have felt that the past Democratic Party, whose motto seemed to be "tax, spend, and get reelected," did some beneficial things for our country, including the G.I. Bill, Medicare, and the Social Security Act, which President Roosevelt signed. Democrats also established unions to protect the working man and fight for child labor laws to protect abused working children, particularly in the 1920s and 1930s of the 20th century.

Today, I largely enjoy my Medicare and Social Security retirement checks now that I am in my "Golden Years." Thank you, Democrats!

But the party has been changing for the last twenty years or so, becoming more socialist and libelous as it tries to direct the world's communications alongside the dominant left-wing media. I blame the huge setback on the Democrats, who did not see it until election day and only suspected it after the November Presidential Debate.

Democrats seem to focus on what is wrong with this country and their lives rather than what is right. They also seem almost unable to overcome their disappointment and outrage, along with a strong desire to fight the Barbarians at the Gate. At every turn, the Right is trying to drag them into a balanced budget, tax reductions to let Americans enjoy more of their own earnings, a war-free world, and, best of all, an economy that encourages new technologies and corporate and foreign investment.

Resistance to lowering the $36 trillion national debt and reluctance to change regulations that impede healthy growth, but no budging from "the party of the people," who would rather fight what the Republicans are trying to do than help the American people.

I'm sure that by now, if I have any liberal readers left, they are dismissing everything I say as a massive delusion concocted by the Republicans and conservative outlets such as Fox News, The Wall Street Journal, the New York Post, and Newsmax.

This is unfortunate because I think understanding what's been laid out here could help them allay the depth of their disappointment and many of their fears about the Trump administration, and help them feel hopeful about the U.S.'s positive future. Recent statistics show the Democrats have lost 2.1 million members, while Republicans have gained 2.4 million, indicating that many of you are starting to peer through the media veil and see the truth.

Chapter 5 | Government

Foreign Policy

The Nuclear Strike Against Iran

On June 21, 2025, after a 60-day warning to Iran, frustration had reached a breaking point. Intelligence sources indicated that Iran was on the verge of developing a devastating nuclear weapon that it would most likely use against Israel, America's key ally in the Middle East, and possibly beyond.

Since 1979, under the rule of the Ayatollahs, Iran has been a key exporter of terrorism and an admitted enemy of the entire non-Muslim world. It has also been Israel's key enemy, and it has resorted to bombing both military installations and civilian centers. Iran has been working on a nuclear weapons program for years, with plans to reach Israel, most of the Mideast, and even parts of Europe. It undoubtedly intended to spread nuclear devastation as far as the US, Europe, and parts of Asia. Small wonder President Trump wanted to render this country "nuclear-free."

He gave the Ayatollah sixty days to come to the negotiating table, a generous diplomatic gesture. Iran showed no interest in peace. After saying he would consider his next step, Trump waited a couple of days, then held off for the next two weeks.

After only two days, precision bombs were dropped on this country's nuclear facilities (with no intent to harm the Iranian people or destroy property, other than their war machine).

Following the strike, Congressional Democrats (whom I still view as an ineffective group in Congress, often sitting on their hands) immediately complained that they hadn't been consulted about the move. If the Democratic Congress had known the details of the secret attack, it would have leaked them to the press.

For example, I am sure that the far-left American members of this body, such as AOC, would have immediately announced it to the press, destroying the surprise and endangering our bomber pilots, our troops, and military installations, including ships in the Strait of Hormuz.

Most of the free world hopes that the Iranian people will take over the country's leadership from the rigid Ayatollah, bring Iran back to the pre-1979 modernization and relative freedom they enjoyed before the Shah was exiled, and find a haven in the United States to treat his life-ending cancer.

Once again, the Democrats are calling for the impeachment of the president, claiming that he violated the War Powers Act of 1973, which regulates the president's use of military force and invasion without congressional approval. In this case, there was no troop invasion, and the strike, if that's what we used, was so exceptionally effective that the altercation with Iran was a devastating blow to their pernicious nuclear attack plans for the future.

I recognize that Democrats' defense strategies are used only to appease, which seems like a naïve concept in the modern world. Undoubtedly, all we will hear from the left-wing media that don't recognize the strategy and precision the president used to avoid all-out war and spare the world from a devastating nuclear capability.

Peace in the Middle East has always seemed an unattainable goal. Now, thirty-five countries have joined Donald Trump to oversee peace between Hamas and Israel. A noble accomplishment by our president, but we should recognize that peace is very difficult to achieve and probably much harder to maintain.

A.I.D.

When I started this book, there was controversy surrounding the A.I.D. program that Trump was trying to abolish. This all sounded about right to me, since I had a terrible experience with this program, or rather, the lack of it, in the 80s.

Two partners and I had structured an agricultural program in Egypt to grow vegetables, irrigating them with water from the Nile's tributaries. Our motto was the ancient proverb: "Give a man a fish, and you feed him for a day. Teach a man to fish, and you feed him for a lifetime."

Raising food inexpensively and shipping it to Europe in winter could be highly profitable, as we would fetch £2 per pound for tomatoes in the U.K., while our cost was five cents per pound plus shipping. We had approximately 40,000 acres dedicated to the project. Our first three years were marred by setbacks of almost biblical proportions:

In the first year, as our John Deere heavy equipment was being shipped to Alexandria, Egypt, to start our project, President Sadat was assassinated. Egyptian officials were unsure whether Egypt would turn away from its U.S. and Western European alliances and possibly return to Russia. As a result, amid uncertainty, they delayed most imports, including our equipment, from being offloaded. We missed the first crop year as our ships sat idle near Alexandria.

In the second year, cholera broke out in the Arab Middle East, and we were prevented from shipping out of the Arab countries. Instead of fetching more than £2 per pound of tomatoes during the European winter, we were restricted to shipping to Middle Eastern countries at five cents per pound, which was less than our cost of goods.

By then, despite setbacks, our project was gaining recognition for its intent, and CBS had produced a TV special featuring my partner in the field in Egypt. The special also featured Presidents Reagan and Mubarak, who visited the project in person and praised it as a model for feeding the world.

With these kudos and international recognition, we were very enthusiastic about our prospects for year three. I had engaged sales agents in Switzerland and England to handle marketing for our products in Europe, and we were ready for a successful year.

Alas, Egypt, a country that has had over 5,000 years to develop its own Bureaucratic Swamp, told us that year, "the man with the Key to the Nile had shut off the many canals and tributaries and had not returned after the allotted two weeks."

Every year, the Nile tributaries were dredged and cleaned, and we expected the canals to be closed for only two weeks. However, due to the added delay and water loss, which extended beyond four weeks, our crops were ruined.

In Washington, desperate for funding, we met with AID, which suggested we contact the U.S. AID representative in Egypt. He had been given over $280 million by AID with no limits and could help with our project. I asked the Egyptian government to help me find the man who had all these dollars. They said they would find him, and I could meet with him and use a small portion of his funds to support our fourth year. Again, there was no U.S. or Egyptian control over the missing Egyptian, as they found out he had left town for Switzerland, accompanied by over a quarter of a billion U.S. dollars. After that, we reached out to every agency, including the World Bank, the State Department, and the U.S. Ambassador to Egypt, who also tried to help us. However, there was no trace of a very wealthy AID recipient living in Switzerland. I was pleased to see that DOGE had already reduced the AID staff by eighty-three percent early this year, deeming them ineffective. I question the seventeen percent remaining. Indeed, this is often the case when the U.S. deals naively with overseas governments.

Waste

Elon Musk has been giving, and continues to give, much of his time and, regrettably, his wealth to help Trump cut overhead in federal offices, which is long overdue. Here is one of the cleverest men in the world, as well as the richest, who has created some of the most technologically advanced companies, yet he is being decried as a selfish multi-billionaire who wants U.S. money for himself.

First, Musk has lost a great deal of his own Tesla equity for every moment he spent helping the United States save itself. For years, not just the Democratic Party but also the Republicans have built out an intricate, overly enthusiastic "spend plan" for the United States. This has taken place over many years. With no spending restrictions when both parties agree, the national debt has now reached $36 trillion and shows no signs of abating unless strong measures are implemented in our system. Elon Musk came in unpaid and losing money daily, as his retail Tesla showrooms were attacked by lawbreakers who either didn't or chose not to understand what Musk was doing for the country. Instead of enriching himself, he has lost at least $65 billion in Tesla stock. God knows how much he has sacrificed by pointing out the huge buildup of nonproductive manpower in our government. His remaining DOGE (Department of Government Efficiency) group was working to provide basic services to all Americans while eliminating a significant portion of the federal government's accumulated bureaucracy. Unfortunately, the major effort has been deferred.

"Efficiency is doing things right.
Effectiveness is doing the right things."

■ *Peter Drucker*

"Move fast and break things." There was fear that the initial zeal of the Trump and Musk efforts to cut waste would result in "throwing the baby out with the bathwater," because their cuts appeared to be based on numbers rather than on competence.

At some point, I believe the White House will have to address the quality of deep government cuts. Of course, many government workers waste time and money and even fail to show up for work, but we should develop a way to identify them while retaining the most accomplished and effective contributors.

To begin, I would establish a standard for identifying effective managers and productive workers using a results-oriented scale. I recognize there is a degree of glee in the White House about reporting the mass termination, but as any management consultant would advise, these cuts should be strategic, not wholesale.

As with any administration, removing people indiscriminately, regardless of their effectiveness or contribution, can have undesirable effects and create chaos, producing the very results they are trying to avoid.

Waste likely developed over hundreds of years, but its intensity has increased in recent years, so it is not an overnight event. Therefore, we must carefully define who is productive, which procedures are effective, and how we can build a safety net by providing this service to our own citizens.

"Chainsaw Al"

Years ago, in the 1960s, there was an individual named "Chainsaw Al Dunlap," who specialized in downsizing organizations and increasing profits. This "turnaround" expert was hired by many major U.S. organizations (including Scott Paper, Crown Zellerbach, Kimberly-Clark, and Lily-Tulip paper cups) to strategically reduce their labor forces and other impediments to profitability. Unfortunately, this renowned expert came a cropper in a massive accounting scandal at Sunbeam Products, which ultimately led to the company's bankruptcy.

Although he was able to move smoothly from company to company, allegedly "cutting their overhead and returning them to profitability" in later years, he was eventually named "one of the ten worst executives in American business history."

Many of his policies also undermined waste-reduction efforts and broader good intentions. Al let people go before he knew their value to the company. He chose quantity over quality, which disrupted the workflow. He did not take the time to understand existing systems, and as a result, he eliminated valuable employees and dismantled effective operations. He failed to implement a management-by-objects (MBO) program, which would have provided executives with clear, measurable expectations aligned with top management's goals. In my opinion, this type of leadership should be avoided in any serious attempt to reduce waste, fraud, and abuse.

Government Vs Industry

Business leaders seem more pragmatic than government managers. They are very concerned with their quarterly performance, spending, and results. For example:

1. They look for any current or future problem and prepare accordingly.
2. They identify personnel weaknesses in the organization and take steps to remove the deadwood as soon as possible. This usually involves reassigning or firing certain individuals who aren't pulling their oar.

3. They are constantly seeking new technologies that may impact their industry and influence product selection, consumer direction, and even new alliances and acquisitions.

4. They aim to increase profits both quarterly and annually, mindful of their many "constituencies," including stakeholders, consumers, the board of directors, and suppliers.

By contrast, expect government leaders to push for larger budgets, expanded personnel, and the growth of their operations—mainly at the expense of the American people. Those in politics seek visibility for their work and pound their chests if they can promote another offshoot of the nanny state to the public.

To me, this means:

Business leaders are well-equipped to juggle several balls in the air at once. They're continuously scanning the horizon for potential problems and opportunities.

As the saying goes, "Workers will do what managers inspect."

After the Biden administration's failures, I think it would be wise to favor more business leaders in our political selections. I include governors here, as they are responsible for P&L, run a state, and oversee its finances and overall performance. I would also include military leaders for their ability to manage, coordinate, plan, and execute on a large scale.

Tariffs

Again, the Democrats are becoming catatonic about tariffs. They are inflationary and will damage relationships between countries. If they had listened to Trump, they would've realized that he was planning to use tariffs as "strategic" moves to bring countries more in line with the tariffs the U.S. now pays.

Currently, most of our trading countries impose higher tariffs on U.S. imports than we do on theirs, for example, as of the first quarter of 2025.

China charged five times the U.S. tariffs

- India 6X U.S. tariffs
- Mexico 3 X U.S. tariffs
- Brazil 6 X U.S. tariffs

EU A VAT of twenty to thirty percent plus tariffs on our car exports, 10% vs 2.5% for car imports into the United States.

This is patently unfair, and if Trump is at all successful in adjusting tariffs on a country-by-country basis and bringing fairness to our overseas trade, we may see many significant positive results, including higher long-term income and profits, many more foreign manufacturing units and companies being set up in the United States, and more jobs for more workers.

This also presents an opportunity to better balance our budget and build more favorable alliances with our trading partners and with ourselves, if handled effectively. All negotiations will require Trump's "Art of the Deal." However, I don't doubt there will be some nervous times as these tariffs work through the system. My only concern is that Trump pushed tariffs before he pushed through his tax cuts, as part of his "Big Beautiful Bill." Tariffs are likely longer-term considerations, whereas tax reductions provide immediate relief that citizens can feel.

Now, after several months of experience with tariffs, it has been found that they may not only bring in a $300 billion surplus in 2025 but also generate as much as $1 trillion a year in the future. Trump was right: Strategically using tariffs can level the playing field and increase profits. They will also increase foreign investment in plants, equipment, and financial assets.

Chapter 6 | Educational Bias

Educational Bias

As most of us suspect, there is a significant discrepancy in how Democrats and Republicans are taught in schools and universities: I drew the statistics from my own college (Yale), which conducted a study in August 2024 titled "Faculty Political Diversity."

Overall Faculty
Republicans 3%
Independents 20%
Democrats 77%

Of the total faculty of 1511 members, 2.71% indicated they were Republicans or conservatives.

Key Departments – Republican representation
African American studies 0
Anthropology 0
Applied Mathematics 4
Architecture 0
Astronomy 0
Biomedical Engineering 8
Chemistry 1
Computer Science 3
Earth/Planetary Science 0
Ecology 0
Economics 0
Electrical and Computer Engineering 0
English 0
History 0

History of Science Medicine 0
Law School 4
Mechanical Engineering 1
Molecular Physics 0
Molecular Biology 2
Philosophy 0
Political Science 1
Psychology 0
Sociology 0
Statistics
Data Science 1

Among all U.S. universities, I thought Yale had a slightly higher proportion of Republicans than the average. Harvard has only 1% of its faculty who admit to being Republicans. Nevertheless, I believe these numbers paint a picture and set a backdrop for who is teaching our children and youth today, what their thought processes are, and who controls the dialogue. There's nothing wrong in and of itself with being a Democratic professor, but with the preponderance of liberal professors, do we not believe that a certain amount of slanted opinions creeps into the discourse and class discussions with these professors?

Notably, Yale Law School, considered one of the finest in the U.S., is represented by only four Republicans out of a total faculty of 106. They are teaching the young men who will move into law firms and will be key figures in our future corporations and judicial courts.

I'm sure this preponderance of Democrats in other fields, such as business, the ABA, politics, and entertainment law, will be a factor in future youth learning experiences. We are now reducing DEI initiatives, which wrongly prioritize diversity over merit.

With near-Machiavellian zeal, the Democratic Party is lining up to obstruct nearly every positive thing President Trump is trying to do.

They are waging a war against the "War on Waste." They seem to recognize that Elon Musk is someone who has come to exploit our country and divert funds to himself. He is obviously in need, as his net worth is only $300 billion. The Democrats figure they cannot learn anything from the richest man in the world, who is guiding us into space exploration and planetary travel despite his recent fallout with Trump. SpaceX is expected to be the largest IPO in 2026.

Democrats claim that our second-term president is ready to scrap Social Security and probably most of Medicare. Yet they fight against efforts to keep the Waste, Fraud, and Abuse operation alive and well, which supports these important services to the country.

They are blaming the recent air crashes earlier in 2025 on the Republicans' efforts to streamline the FAA and reduce the number of government personnel, including air traffic controllers. I understand they have not fired any air traffic controllers, but they are facing a significant shortage, as most seasoned controllers are seeking early retirement at age fifty-five. In a quote from Delta Air Lines' CEO, he claims that air controllers are not a factor. On the contrary, one of the few government shortages in the United States is the number of air traffic controllers, as these are extremely high-pressure, mid-level pay jobs with millions of lives at stake, and they are truly the masters of our safety in the blue skies.

Despite their blind spots, liberals remain highly creative in countering and dismissing Trump's effort to fix the country by spreading untruths and misinterpreting the news.

They geared up to destroy Trump's effort to pass one big bill that would eliminate open borders, reduce taxes, restore our energy dominance, and eventually reduce our incredibly high national debt from the current $36 trillion. Using "LIE-WARE," I believe the Democrats' overall intent is to defeat or undermine Trump's plans so that, in the midterms, they control Congress once again and thereby return to their motto of "tax, spend, and be re-elected," and, incidentally, move us closer to moral decay, like Gomorrah. Hopefully, their next candidates for a major election will understand where past administrations have gone astray and become more pragmatic and pro-American. But insider power and profits continually loom large for legislators. The name "The Democratic Party" no longer seems to stand for efforts on behalf of the people's welfare, but only to enhance its own members' interests.

I've heard that the Department of Education has a $75,000-per-teacher overhead budget in the U.S. Returning this function to the states brings parents closer to the organizations and to a local syllabus, giving them greater power in education and closer alignment with what they need for their children. The

Department of Education has existed since Jimmy Carter's presidency and has expanded educational programs and increased funding for the unions.

I don't think teachers set out to instill hate in their students, but it appears to be a byproduct of their own beliefs, as emphasized in nearly all their lectures and historical interpretations, whether the nation's founding is considered 1619 or 1776.

Yet certain Democrats still object to eliminating red tape and want to continue the annual increase in swampy overhead, not only in education but also in most other government departments.

Americans on both sides of the aisle should applaud Musk and his generous, perhaps somewhat idealistic, efforts to bring our entire government into line. This cannot be done without some limitations and, possibly, personal tragedies for those who must be moved or removed from their current homes and jobs. This has been achieved in part through the early retirement of thousands, transfers for others, and orders requiring government workers to return to their offices daily. I personally believe that many of these so-called 'government workers' are moonlighting in second jobs, likely in private industry, while still collecting a government paycheck for doing little or nothing.

Black Lives Matter wants reparations for enslaved families and payback for White Supremacy. While some Christians rant, "Jews killed Jesus" and should "face eternal punishment if not extermination."

These are all seductive discussions in many school lessons to a greater or lesser degree, but the overall conclusion is that schools today, including universities, and specific studies also teach the validity of certain humans over others, perhaps comforting to some, but usually erroneous.

Across school boards, efforts are now being made, to varying degrees, to cease antisemitism in their schools and to eliminate DEI, but both have apparently been growing trends in the recent century.

School boards have been favoring grade escalation, and passing appears to be the rule rather than failure for almost all kids. Kids are pushed along because it's more trouble to leave them back. Students now have time on their hands to express their opinions, but not to learn the root causes or historical reasons for their prejudices. I mentioned a 2024 study conducted at my own university on faculty politics at Yale, which found that only three percent of Yale's faculty identify as conservative or Republican. The rest are various levels of liberal socialism or the far left. This has led to an increasingly socialist society as these young people graduate and leave the academic world to populate law firms, large corporations, research centers, and, in fact, every walk of life, bringing with them a socialist mindset they learned in college.

This raises the old chestnut: "If you're not a liberal at twenty-four, you have no heart, and if you're not a conservative by forty-four, you have no brain."

Chapter 7 | Democrats

Democracy and Truth

In truth, the Republicans have had a pretty good 2024-2025 and can therefore afford to lie less and manipulate the news less. But to be fair, the right-wing media, although limited in number, are ready to pounce if they perceive conveniently constructed stories from CNN, MSNBC, CNBC, the New York Times, and social media, such as:

- The Russian Collusion syndrome with Trump.
- Hunter Biden's laptop was suppressed just before the 2020 election.
- That President Biden was fully mentally competent.
- Trump is a despot and will rule like one.
- The Biden family is honest and has never had any personal financial deals with China, Russia, or any foreign entity.
- The Green Lobby (which ignores climate-saving nuclear energy and LNG) will save the planet environmentally (but ruin it economically).
- That Kamala "Do Nothing" Harris is a great candidate to continue Biden's policies. She has stated that she agrees with everything he has done or said.
- China has had no part in U.S. politics, and despite owning TikTok, it is not poisoning young minds and gathering harmful data as Republicans suggest.

- The unfortunate withdrawal from Afghanistan was the fault of the U.S. generals, not Biden.
- We need illegal immigrants for agriculture, even though currently, only a handful of these undocumented immigrants have farming, agricultural, or even domestic jobs.

I agree that Fox News and similar outlets too often over-praise Trump's actions without criticizing his sometimes crude demeanor, but he's generally on the mark.

Other questionable practices exposed:
There has been an effort by some groups to eliminate traditional gender identity. This manifests in two ways:

a) The controversial notion of allowing biological men to compete in women's sports. Although 79% of Americans oppose it, it persists in some areas, notably in Maine, where the governor still refuses to enforce the separation of the sexes in sports.
b) The practice of performing irreversible procedures on young boys and girls reflects a troubling effort to eliminate sexual distinction. I am frankly at a loss to understand where this stems from or where it is going (hopefully, nowhere). I recently heard a radio broadcast featuring a young man, now twenty-four, who described being castrated at age seven for gender transition—a decision he did not choose. He was nearly in tears because he can no longer be a boy, procreate, or marry a girl. Whoever caused this to

happen ruined this young man's life by depriving him of his manhood. Even considering that this could be a practice in the United States is beyond reason. What is wrong with these people?

c) This fringe group has also advocated for language changes to somehow strengthen their cases. One suggestion was to replace the words "Mother" or "Granny" with the term "impregnated one."

Can you see yourself at a family get-together where you must call your grandmother, your wife, and your married daughter "impregnated ones?"
I suspect much of this stems from the ability to communicate a wide range of unusual terms, phrases, and beliefs prevalent on social media.

I am not saying extremists are primarily Democrats, as there seems to be a universal tendency among certain groups in our country to adopt and use these unbalanced tactics, regardless of party.

Democratic Decorum

I am deeply disappointed by the Democratic response to Trump's agenda. There doesn't appear to be any effort to understand what Trump is driving at, and there's an automatic negative reaction to his principles, objectives, and methods.

After all, Trump has identified a serious problem with our government's staffing and spending and is trying to restore productivity, balance the budget, and close our borders to what he sees as the most insidious threat to America and its institutions.

Liberal Party Plans

I keep thinking of Reagan's vision of "a city on a hill" and believe there is hope in America, and that the Democrats will stop their moping and become an important part of our growth.

It is hard to do it alone, particularly given their mindless blocking of many planned improvements. They are not blocking Republicans' suggested rule changes out of superior knowledge, but simply to stop Trump in his tracks, no matter how favorable and productive his ideas for our country are, and thereby leaving our citizens in the lurch.

Overall, their strategy is to counter and demean Trump's spending plans, bills, the Department of Government Efficiency (DOGE), the government, and his waste reduction program, as well as his foreign policy, while keeping their voters focused on what they portray as the "disasters" of the Trump presidency.

They continually attempt to repeat this narrative, utilizing every available communicative channel.

Other Anticipated Actions by Democrats:

- Obstruction of bills, motions, or actions put forward by Trump.
- Use the democratic-leaning press to shed negative light on the current GOP plans.
- Use LIE-WARE to put forward an alternative truth to each day's events.
- Use Law-Fare to eliminate all Trump programs, especially the Big Beautiful Bill and government cuts.

• Use local federal judges to stop or stall any new Trump bills and try to incarcerate the president.

• Use dramatics and emotion to depict the plight of illegal immigrants (while ignoring the huge expense of maintaining and supporting this group).

Try to demean all GOP activities, focusing on:

1. Ridiculous attempts by Trump to control Mexico, Iran, Canada, China, Venezuela, Greenland, and others through inflation-building tactics.

2. Put pressure on and, in some cases, eliminate institutions that have backed Trump in the past, including the NRA, selected unions, police forces, and DOGE.

3. Also, fight Trump's attempt to wage a war against waste in what I call, *wage-a-war-against-a-war-against-waste.*

4. Continually attack Trump's Cabinet actions and push to pack the courts, particularly the United States Supreme Court, with liberal judges.

5. Use of the lower courts to frustrate the White House's legal efforts, employing Lawfare to confound them.

6. Use the court system, where possible, to freeze, suspend, or deny any Trump programs, and renew efforts to pack the courts and protect the U.S. Supreme Court from the GOP's effort to control the government.

7. Undertake a massive campaign to fight ICE and defend the poor illegal refugees who came here out of desperation. These groups are now being incarcerated in either the former torture center, Guantánamo, or the Alligator Alcatraz in the Florida

Everglades, or repatriated to their troubled countries, or worse.

8. Illustrate the illegal separation of families and the hardships poor immigrants and their children endure.

9. Forge even stronger relationships with mass media, social media, liberal newspapers and magazines, and television networks.

10. Use technology (e.g., AI) wherever possible to have the Democratic story seep into every news crevice and help the public understand the Trump threat, especially during the midterms, when the Democrats aim to take back the House, if not the Senate.

11. Contest tax-lowering efforts as costly, inflationary, and intended to reward the very rich.

12. Be aware of any Republican misstep and publicize any lapse in judgment or decorum.

13. Vilify the members of the Trump Cabinet as rich, questionable choices who are only interested in enriching themselves.

14. And if they can't do the above truthfully, use LawFare and LIE-WARE, along with their cooperative left-wing press, to get our story out there.

15. Try to anticipate any Trump triumph, such as the successful bombing of Iran, with alternate accounts of cruelty, nation-building, or destruction.

The above is what I suspect the Liberal Democrats plan for the Trump years. As events unfold, they will continue to employ the same LIE-WARE tactics they have used for years. The effect will be to continue isolating liberal thinkers from GOP progress and from truth in reporting.

Unfortunately, these objectives will keep most Democrats mired in gloom and leave nearly half of the United States in despair, worry, and fear—not only for the next four years but also for their children's long-term future under what they call leadership by "an insane Nazi billionaire."

Media Stars

There appear to be several highly paid media "talents" who earn large sums by claiming to broadcast objectively while lying about the Trump administration and the MAGA way of life.

For example, there is Rachel Maddow, who is rumored to earn $30 million a year for a once-a-week broadcast in which she directs invective at Trump and the GOP. She also passes along hearsay and rarely acknowledges any progress the current administration is making, instead cutting, cauterizing, and molding her comments to fit her inflexible beliefs. There is The View, where four or five liberal ladies scream about Trump being the most evil man alive.

Anderson Cooper, another liberal CNN commentator, earns $20 million a year. Fortunately for him, he is a direct descendant of Cornelius Vanderbilt and a successful writer, which puts him in a position to supplement his CNN salary if it diminishes. He represents a modest improvement over Maddow but still closely aligns with the positions he hears from the Democratic Party's left wing.

The Swamp

After three months of Trump's second term, many Democrats now seem to hate their own Senate Majority Leader, Schumer, in March 2025, even more than they hate Trump. In our screwed-up world, Schumer is being vilified for once doing the right thing. There is never a good reason to shut down the government, regardless of political intent. When Democrats had Republicans in the same position, facing a CR, Republicans all vowed that saving the country, keeping payments to our service members, continuing Social Security checks, and maintaining Medicare coverage were more important than virtually closing the country. Schumer agreed. Now the shoe was on the other foot, and in March 2025, Schumer had to make the brave, unpopular move to keep the country going, earning him a pariah label from his own party. How is this for Double Speak? Now, in October and again in February 2026, Schumer has backtracked and supports a government shutdown, in part to save his Senate seat.

It is striking to me that the blue party would prefer to cut off financial support to all its constituents, its armies, and even its retirees for forty-three days to suppress the opposing party. The disarrayed Democrats seem willing to sacrifice moral, ethical, and legal considerations if it means undermining Trump—even at the expense of their own country.

Most of the swamp denizens have never had any true financial responsibility for anything, never had to meet a payroll, never had to risk their own money on a project, and never had to fire or "clean out" any organization or industry. Yet they have consistently advocated for continued waste, as this dissolute spending gets them elected and reelected under the guise of spending for their fellow man, which is light-years from the truth. Earlier, I highlighted the distinction between the business leader's mentality and the objectives of swamp leaders. During my five years in Washington, DC (I never held a government job), however, our efforts to technologically perfect TV 'streaming' were largely backed by the Department of Defense, which foresaw 'streaming' as a defensive weapon, enabling instantaneous communication worldwide. Although most of these people were well-meaning, I did not see the urgency or the incisive questioning that business leaders would have demanded before investing over $1 million in the project. Perhaps salaries should be based on merit, positive results, and the achievement of agreed-upon objectives, rather than on how quickly one can expand an organization and accumulate unnecessary personnel. In Washington, I lived near a highly regarded government financial manager who would often see me from his patio as I arrived back from work at eight o'clock or later. He would ask me why I had to stay so late. I said I had more work to do. He looked puzzled and said, 'Why don't you do it tomorrow?' It would be hard to explain that by tomorrow, I would have twenty other key challenges to solve.

Is it possible, with a clean budget confirmed each year and the elimination of waste that Trump is seeking, to eliminate CRs entirely? But only if we can have a clean budget approved by both parties and not used by either party as a total political lever? This is a worthwhile objective and may be one of the byproducts of Trump's plans. I hope so.

Higher Taxes

The intellectual world has long discussed the population crisis. The Malthusian Theory holds that population growth increases geometrically, whereas food production grows arithmetically. This imbalance, he argues, will lead to "natural" checks on population growth through famine, disease, and vice. About the same time, Johnathan Swift wrote his satirical essay, *A Modest Proposal.*

- He proposed that poor Irish children, rather than being a burden, should be raised for consumption by the wealthy class.
- He argues that this would solve the problem of poverty, ease the burden on parents, and even provide them with some income.

The world continues to be concerned about population growth, but the factors have changed and are just as pressing:

- People are living longer
- Couples are having fewer children
- Youth departure from their countries.

Russia's Rosstat projects that its youth population will decline by 130 million by 2056, in no small part due to the war in Ukraine, which has devastated both Ukrainians and Russians. They are suffering from a

Vietnam-type attitude, particularly among young men disillusioned with their Mother Country.

For us, fewer young people mean fewer retirement funds in the U.S. When Social Security was established in 1935, there were approximately 40 to 160 workers for every retiree. Today, there are fewer than three workers for every retiree, and this ratio continues to decline. This is one reason Social Security will be in jeopardy in the next few years and will be "broken" by 2035.

It seems clear to me that some changes will be necessary. The ultra-conservatism that has governed Social Security investments over the last century has been a contributing factor—arguably appropriate, given the importance of safeguarding retirement savings. However, a combination of a higher eligibility age and stricter oversight of waste and staffing will provide a temporary solution for the system, with an emphasis on technological growth (à la FAANG stocks).

Social Security

Once again, Democrats are conflating the removal of waste and excess government workers with the reduction of Social Security and Medicare benefits. There is considerable waste, dishonesty, and deception in the disbursement of these funds, particularly within the Social Security Administration. For example, a single Social Security number can be linked to more than 100 addresses and still receive monthly checks. Some of these recipients are listed as over 140 years old.

They do not comprehend that if the United States is successful in reducing government waste, then the benefits and stability of government for the American people will be on a safer footing.

Cuts in unnecessary personnel and streamlining processes are different from cutting benefits.

In fact, I've long believed that if we put a portion of Social Security savings into the stock market or other instruments, such as the bitcoin explosion, there will be a double benefit to the country: the economy will be boosted, and funds for retirees will be greatly increased, which can be used to fund future retirees instead of raising the age almost annually. The stock market has generated a seven-and-a-half percent return over the last fifty years, while restricted Social Security investments have generated just over one percent. This spread has widened in the past decade.

Consequently, there's bound to be a squeeze as our birth rates decline, leaving fewer young people to support their retiring elders. For years, this has been a government option that Democrats have addressed with fear and trembling. "What if the market goes down just as an individual is retiring? His benefits could be greatly reduced."

To my mind, this could be countered by averaging three to four years of prior market performance to mitigate declines in the retiring year. Over time, the risk is minimal; however, in any given year, Social Security funds could experience a sharper decline during down markets. I believe there will be an explosion, particularly in technologies such as supercomputers, AI, ChatGPT, Super AI, space, and other emerging technologies, which will undoubtedly revolutionize how we live, heal, work, amuse, and spend our time. The Social Security Administration will have to figure out how to smooth the vagaries of the market so retirement will not keep our aging Americans awake at night. After age sixty-seven, in down-market years, they can access a portion of their funds, deferring the bulk of their account until retirement at age seventy. If up to twenty percent of funds were allocated to alternative investments, such as bitcoin, technology stocks, crucial raw materials, IPOs, and precious metals, returns could improve significantly. Perhaps the SS administration could consider using successful private fund managers or fiduciaries for a portion of their pool, thereby representing dynamic growth and adding immeasurably to the benefits of retirees in the future, thereby alleviating some of the pressure the Social Security Administration faces today.

Currently, I believe that vast new growth industries, particularly those in technology, AI, and the IPO sector, should be included in the Social Security investment portfolio. Of course, a three-year adjustment before or after the retirement date could help smooth the results.

Belief Systems

When I was born, eons ago, the U.S. was a faithful nation. Most people attended church or synagogue regularly; most children were taught to say "Now I Lay Me Down to Sleep" at bedtime; and most schools recited the Pledge of Allegiance each morning. Recently, we have become more materialistic, a little less patriotic, and "too sophisticated" to believe the Bible and its stories, which are really parables. It's almost a fashion to deny any system or faith. I believe this results in a less happy, less healthy populace.

Life expectancy, health, and general happiness among believers surpass those of non-believers.

One example: it is hard for me to believe that the Big Bang occurred without any impetus or cause. Just about every scientist believes in "cause and effect." These same learned gentlemen also line up, almost to a man, against the spontaneous Big Bang Theory, which presents an 'effect' without a 'cause.' Go figure!

The majority of scientists today believe in a universe that simply grew "like Topsy."

These men are ready to tell us everything about our lives. They can explain its origins and how it functions, yet they still have no concept of how it started. Embracing the Big Bang Theory does not necessarily mean you are a person of faith, but it's a start.

So, Democrats, you can remain mired in self-pity, fear, and lack of confidence in your government.

Or—you can try to see both sides of the news, be alert to Lie-Ware from either party, and view Trump (and his administration) as a tough leader with the chops to move the United States aggressively away from the suicidal direction the previous White House seemed to prefer. He has made clear efforts to reduce a bloated government, take responsibility for restarting and securing energy independence, curb inflation, fix the border through selective enforcement, improve trade practices, and achieve orderly repatriation of undocumented immigrants.

I personally find the idea of a loving, caring being overseeing our fates far more satisfying than being an atheist with little hope after death or little value in prayer. I'm sure there are many liberals and possibly others who renounce my thesis—that if you are leaning toward spirituality, you are also leaning toward conservatism, the rule of law, pragmatic solutions, and, deep down, the potential goodness of man. Even AA insists that recognizing a higher being is necessary for achieving alcohol-free success.

Years ago, when we were children, we were told to avoid discussing politics and religion. Yes, discussions of these elements of human life often foment arguments, disdain for the other person's belief system, and, frankly, they are never really resolved. However, having said that, you can live with some faith or continue your troubled life, shaped by LIE-WARE, and live in permanent outrage like Bernie Sanders.

"'Tis a tangled web we weave when first we practice to deceive."

--Shakespeare

Meanwhile, removing deadwood and illegal activities, plus streamlining the processes that run Social Security, will also benefit the economy and the safety of these programs.

Similarly, in January 2005, Vice President Dick Cheney said, "In fact, young workers who elect personal accounts can expect to receive a far higher rate of return on their money, 7.4 percent (now ten percent), than the current Social Security system could ever afford to pay them."

Example: If a twenty-five-year-old invested $1,000 per year for forty years at Social Security's top rate of return, she would have over $125,000. But if she invested the money in the stock market, earning even its lowest historical rate of return, she would earn more than double that amount, or $250,000.

Cato, the Heritage Foundation, and several other organizations that support private accounts also routinely claim to achieve ten percent returns.

Now, imagine if she invested $1,000 per month at a ten percent annual interest rate. She would have a nest egg of over $500,000 in forty years. Her outlook would be dramatically better. Social Security should consider this kind of measure if the birth rate remains low or continues to decline.

If you embrace a bit of faith, you'll be happier, less traumatized, and feel better about your children's prospects and our country's leadership. So pursue the truth; it will make you and most of the world FREE!

The alternative is a state of gloom and doom. As you feel our country is abandoned by any sensible leadership, you continue to fall prey to the false allegations of a future errant government that will drive us toward war, advocate reducing government workers and increasing the deficit, bloat the government, and turn its back on energy independence, generally driving us to disaster.

"Anyone who is capable of getting themselves made President should on no account be allowed to do the job."

Douglas Adams:
Hitchhiker's Guide to the Galaxy 1979.

"Politics, as a practice, whatever its professions, has always been the systematic organization of hatreds. Practical politics consists of ignoring facts."

The Education of Henry Adams (1907)
Henry Adams, 1838-1918

On the media side, Scott Pelley, speaking at a Wake Forest commencement, offered the world insight into the errant mind of a longtime newsman. He spewed invective at Trump, saying he was leading us pell-mell into disaster. He seemed to lose his mind over the issues and what those monsters in the White House are doing to our people. On the plus side, he summed up the damage the Democrats have done to us, including the damage from Biden's first-day actions, which have not yet been fully assessed, and came close to destroying our nation and relegating the country to financial decline and Third World status.

However, Scott apparently was unaware of any concerns about President Biden's cognitive or physical fitness and felt that everything would be fine if we continued the open-border policy and halted our energy dominance. He apparently, in his own mind, is an innocent dupe when it comes to knowing the true condition of Biden, but that's OK, because he still accurately followed a liberal or collectivist manifesto that the mainstream media was trying to foist on us.

The ceremony underscored how polarized our public discourse has become. Graduates left shaken or inspired, depending on their views, and the address quickly became fodder for both praise and condemnation across the political spectrum. To many, the prospect of a positive future seemed doubtful, and the event ended with anger and disrespect for elected leaders.

It is hard to believe, but the LIE-WARE (disinformation tactics) employed by the media appears to have clouded the minds of journalists themselves. I accuse them of relying heavily on LIE-WARE and then treating it as some truth to be proclaimed.

This is one reason many Democrats and other voters went for Kamala. The Democratic media are spreading doom, and they have misled their people into thinking our country is in malicious hands and that the salvation of our citizens is remote.

During President Trump's speech to Congress in March, he focused on the accomplishments he and his administration had achieved, which were considerable, but the key thing I took away was the image of the entire Democratic Congress sitting on their hands, looking like a log pile, and not appearing ready to accomplish anything positive for this country. You would think that, after four years of Biden, which was a real setback for our country, they would be more apologetic and throw themselves into reform to counter the devastation wrought by the prior White House.

Instead, they sat there, cheerless and ready to promote their discouraging, dark world, where LIE-WARE and Law-Fare have shaped much of their opinions, actions, and fears.

All the feelings I once had for the Democratic Party, which I once admired (admittedly from a distance), have now turned into a naysayer party.

The former party of the people has forgotten the people and stands in unity against reducing taxes and against removing illegal aliens expeditiously, but it seems they are plunging our country into despair and financial disaster.

They did some good things years ago, despite their avowed purpose of "tax and spend" (and I add - "get reelected"), which still prevails. But now they appear to be a party in despair and wonderment, clearly like deer in the headlights, so all they can do is savage Trump and his policies instead of gloriously taking up the banner of the restoration of the United States of America and its citizens.

If they ever come to reason and hold one pragmatic belief, they could join the current government to make not only the United States but the world a better place to live in: financially, healthier, by wiping out poverty and crime, and by choosing to fund the police rather than defund them, which, along with our borders, has now formed a disastrous circular firing squad where no one gets out safely, peacefully, or hopelessly, or … alive.

Sanctuary Cities

The Democrats are also the party of the short-sighted when it comes to city and state sanctuaries. Apparently, they do not realize the eventual state they are creating, in which illegal aliens, especially wrongdoers, will be attracted to sanctuaries, virtually immune from prosecution, while bringing higher crime rates, desperation, poverty, and hatred, not to mention the huge local expenses to underwrite these people.

Do sanctuary governors and mayors have any concern for the overall effect of sanctuary policies on their residents' safety? Do they realize that high-income, tax-paying citizens will soon move away from sanctuary areas to escape crime, brutality, and chaos, as well as the carrying costs of these states and towns? Yet the mayors and governors of the major liberal cities stand united in supporting sanctuary policies for their residents and their jurisdictions.

As I write, I suspect "Give me your tired and your poor, your huddled masses yearning to be free" will change to: "Give me your criminals, your scofflaws, your lazy, your dangerous, your mentally ill, your murderers, your sexual offenders," which together constitute the dregs of the world, and we will take care of them—at least until our swollen budgets can no longer pay for enforcement and necessary increases in our services, such as medical, education, hospitalization, police, facilities, and jails. At that point, the burden will become so unsupportable that they will awake and rue their thinking.

Those immigrants who have good jobs and integrate into our society, lured by the promise of a haven, should have the supreme hope that every American can learn to save and support hard-working, productive immigrants while eliminating criminals and the desperate from our shores.

I also think deporting undocumented immigrants should be prioritized.

Those with paying jobs should be allowed to remain a little longer, or until they have a path to citizenship. I also think Dreamers without criminal records are now living in fear of being abruptly torn from their homes and sent to countries they have never set foot in. This will serve as ammunition for many heart-on-sleeve liberals, who will portray it as Republican cruelty and a violation of human rights.

I have long wondered whether anything in our government, the Constitution, or the Declaration of Independence could have prevented President Biden's wayward actions. His record led or encouraged his followers to embrace major setbacks for our country, including the end of energy independence and the halt to exploration for new energy sources. He also oversaw policies that, in my view, contributed to 20,000,000 undocumented immigrants.

Aside from the 25th Amendment, I believe there should be a safety net when a president deviates from their course and begins to harm the country—a clear process for their removal from office.

We have Amendment 25, established to protect the nation in the event the president loses life, health, or capacity. However, it appears that the amendment's mechanisms were not designed to address the kind of gradual or subtle capacity decline that some fear may occur, as witnessed in recent cases.

I believe a simple annual memory test should be mandatory for the President, congressional leaders, and cabinet members. These impartial tests, conducted by a bicameral panel of medical experts, would not be disclosed publicly unless the panel concluded that removal was necessary. They should not be used as political ammunition. Grounds for discharge or even punishment should be rare, narrowly defined, and handled through a transparent, constitutionally grounded process to protect the nation.

Democrats Outlook

Recent observations of the Democrats suggest they are mostly a sad bunch. They lost the election. A recent study reports that fifty-seven percent feel depressed and anxious. Only nineteen percent of Republicans feel that way. It has also been recorded that conservatives live longer than liberals and are healthier, happier, and more spiritual. This has been a factor for both parties in the past, but the Democrats are absolutely convinced that their country is now run by a satanic maniac who, in addition to enriching himself, will call for martial law, thereby using the military to take over the government of the United States, resulting in a police state run by Trump's personal oligarchy. (King for Life?)

For example, the New York Times has spent over twenty years campaigning to undermine, criticize, demean, and vilify Trump as a hot-tempered egomaniac and woman-hating Playboy who wants America to become his personal domain. I once told a friend that if I had been reading the New York Times for the past twenty-plus years, I probably wouldn't have voted for Trump either, because it was so negative and full of LIE-WARE. In this way, the mainstream media was able to sway public opinion negatively for years, and Democrats turned to them for reassurance. Imagine their shock and disappointment when what they believed was mostly the truth from liberal media turned out to be largely untrue. This likely did not improve their comfort or understanding.

We have cited multiple examples of how the left-wing's extensive use of Lie-Ware and Law-Fare was able to warp and reshape the facts and keep the country's awareness from:

1. The negative state of Biden's overall health and mental acuity.
2. How the unlimited influx of undocumented aliens would benefit the workforce, since farms and manufacturers need additional workers to grow.
3. How Kamala Harris was a totally ineffective vice president serving as border Czar. How her experience as Attorney General of the poorly run state of California could help her run the United States. How she clearly doesn't have enough bandwidth to be the most important and powerful person in the world.
4. How the "green lobby" was necessary and how they were using incentives and Lawfare to push fossil-fuel cars off the road.
5. How there was much less 'waste' among our government workers in Washington than the Department of Government Efficiency (DOGE) reported, and how incensed you should be at the indiscriminate firing of good-hearted, hard-

working government employees (when they do show up for work).

6. How good it was that we stopped fracking, exploration, and pipelines from further polluting our world's atmosphere.
7. How regulations could be used by the government to prevent further pollution, protect oil surveys and development, and protect the Delta Smelt.
8. How soon before Ohio will be on the Atlantic, and the eastern seaboard will be flooded by the Atlantic due to global warming?
9. How the Biden White House was doing a great job of keeping inflation down, and that any uptick was "transitory."
10. How the fake 2020 story about Hunter Biden's laptop was a case of Russian collusion with Trump and the start of the term TDS (Trump derangement syndrome).

Plus, other manufactured stories to amuse or outrage Republicans and to reassure, calm, and placate Democrats.

In particular, ladies of the Democratic Party, look more skeptically and carefully at your favorite media's distortions.

In other words, my recommendation, particularly for our Democratic ladies, is to recognize that Trump is not a madman trying to push our country toward ruin. But the last administration was the worst ever, and it may take us decades to recoup.

Trump's personality is very strong, and he often offends with his exaggerations. However, being strong is better than being weak-minded, as we have seen.

Also, expose yourself to other points of view. For example, tune into FOX part-time, say ten percent of your news time (which is not blameless for inflating the news), but it has a more accurate record than CNN, MSNBC, CNBC, or other purveyors of liberal thought. This will provide some balance, as Fox tends to present a more favorable picture of the U.S. and offers a different, if not better, newscast.

It will give you more confidence in our country, our current President, and the White House. We admit his personality is not for everyone, but I would rather have a strong, decisive president who is forceful and negotiates through the Art of the Deal than a smiling, appease-everybody Milquetoast who would rather back down than get along.

And that is what we have, a strong, strategic-minded leader. So, be patient, my friends to the left, and strive to be happier and more spiritual.

Hopefully, your party can, over time, return to being more of an 'instrument for the people' as it was a generation ago.

"In politics, if you want anything said, ask a man. If you want anything done, ask a woman."

--Margaret Thatcher – 1975

Chapter 8 | Progression of LieWare

Media, social media, Law firms, Schools, Grammar to law, Chinese Propaganda

Media, social media, law firms, schools, grammar schools, and Chinese propaganda. Is it possible, with a clean budget confirmed each year and the elimination of waste that Trump is seeking, to eliminate panicked CRs entirely and prevent their use by each party as a form of political leverage? This is a worthwhile objective and may be a byproduct of what Trump is planning. I hope so. Pushing the end of the filibuster could have long-term effects if a Democratic majority were to pack the courts by adding two new states and four Democratic senators (i.e., control of Congress). So care is required in making such a move. Meanwhile, at the time of this writing, the government is closed, thanks to Senate Majority Leader Chuck Schumer, who is using an ineffective temporary COVID-19 healthcare grant as an excuse.

Dear Democrats, think of the difference in our lives… I have seen many administrations over the years, and this is by far the best, thanks to Donald Trump. It makes me happy to see the progress he is making in the Middle East and the Far East, and in confronting our enemies, including China, Russia, Iran, and Hamas, both at home and abroad. I sense we are now becoming a nation at our strongest, and if we could bring this realization to you, you would also be happier, more loyal and discerning, at peace, and less angry and depressed.

However, you are a member of a party in which "Lie-Ware" has been fostered and spread by so-called elite media to put you in a state of permanent gloom and doom, including claims about Nazi leaders, the deprivation of healthcare for our citizens, and illegal, martial-like entries into sanctuary cities. War-like overtures to Hamas and Iran, China, and Russia could be a detriment rather than a move toward world peace. It seems that, on balance, if there's any truth in these statements, it has been inflated by anti-Republican sentiment.

Unbeknownst to you, we have a President who faces world problems with good judgment, is not afraid to take action where needed, and sees illegal immigration and crime as a major potential threat to our country. Yes, I watch Fox News, but I also watch CNN and Meet the Press, and I read The New York Times, The Washington Post, and The Wall Street Journal. From this diverse array of sources, I draw my conclusions, which I have presented in this book. The media can be a force for good or evil, and it has been used for centuries to shape humanity's thoughts and actions. But never has the media been so predominantly left-socialist as it is today, as it fights a battle against progress, peace, and human respect.

Clean Air Lobby

The Biden effort to save the world from pollution and global warming has been largely debunked; there are still large groups of people who constitute the 'green lobby.'

It has been shown that providing energy for both windmills and solar requires large amounts of fossil fuels to get the process started. China is adding new coal plants weekly; meanwhile, our entire energy effort has been handcuffed by Biden's move against exploration, fracking, drilling (onshore and offshore), and LNG (liquid natural gas).

Now "dig, baby, dig!" has rung out, and our energy is rising once again.

Unfortunately, as I looked back in history, nuclear energy has had an exceedingly bad reputation. The world has experienced at least three near-disasters involving nuclear power. But today, nuclear power is much more manageable and safer. Small nuclear generators can light a town, while larger plants have better controls and should be a source of energy embraced by all Americans.

It will be up to the White House and the nuclear development sector to determine how quickly conversion to nuclear fuel can be made. Obviously, this should be a light-speed event, with appropriate regulations and backing from both government and corporate sectors.

Meanwhile, sea levels are not rising. In recent years, the scientific community has largely embraced incidents promoted by the New York Times to advance the liberal warming agenda. However, Hessel Voortman published a paper indicating that "sea level rise across the low-lying Dutch Coast had not accelerated." He then tested this theory at 200 weather stations with at least sixty years of data.

Anthony Blair, reporting on this data in late 2025, concluded that there was no detectable acceleration in sea-level rise. These findings contradicted the UN climate panel, the IPCC, and the New York Times, which had significantly projected large sea-level rises as a 'fact certain' for political purposes and to scare voters into voting Democratic.

Climate of Hate

The human being, going back forever, has been, if not obsessed, at least partially concerned by hate. The individual who has used hate as an important aspect of life, such as the man who was jealous of his neighbor. The tribe living on the east side of the river versus the "awful people living on the west side of the river."

The countries that are envious of a neighboring country yet maintain trade relations with it.

Antisemitism, white supremacy, even the religions that are supposed to bring peace and happiness, are often consumed by hateful cries, "those Catholics or Muslims or Jews or Protestants or Black Lives Matter."

Hate is as old as mankind; it will never be totally eradicated. In my long life, I have witnessed various hates and prejudices, but one of my concerns is a fairly recent one, namely that hate is not only spread by the media but often encouraged by the schools: Antisemitism, or in many cases 'Anti-Israel,' prevails despite the fact that this is a tiny country with its diverse ethnic backgrounds, and it stands as a bulwark against the teeming, massive, and troubled Middle East.

I'm not sure how Lie-Ware can ever be changed to any meaningful degree. Still, as today's youth grow more pragmatic, I hope they will see through it. Tomorrow will reveal things more clearly. Voters will seek the truth even as the elite and social media continue to reconstruct the "truth," and we recognize that truths can be manufactured to promote various party affiliations and ideologies. I've said repeatedly that the left-wing press has not done a great service to their party or their country. The media coverups of the Biden administration, the weakness of the last Democratic candidate for president in 2024, the unlimited importation of illegal aliens over the Biden years, and the reduction in our energy self-sufficiency have made half the population in the country extremely unhappy and uneasy with both their lot in life and the future of their country. On the other hand, I see that the conservative media may have resulted in a gloating party that is over-exuberant and probably unaware of the many pitfalls our country faces in the next few years.

Think of a country without prejudice, hate, Law-Fare, and Lie-Ware. Where all parties seem to want their country's welfare to prevail. Where politicians suggest and work with their opponents to move the "beneficial" ball forward. Together, they promote growth and better policies. To create a country that can offer free healthcare to all. Where homelessness doesn't exist. Where schools teach and teach well. Where there is a comprehensive immigration policy, a balanced budget, and a working healthcare program.

I'm afraid this is a long-term plan that wouldn't yield benefits for several years, but it could be a real positive force in our youth's mindset as they face life with greater assurance, confidence, and focus, and hopefully less prejudice.

The major enemies of our country's progress now appear to be China, Russia, Iran, and the Democratic Party. This might seem contradictory—that belonging to a party that has contributed so much to America would now be in the enemy column—but they appear willing to use LawFare and anything else to stop Trump in his tracks and hold back progress. They have portrayed his efforts as inimical to the country's interests.

Many have lambasted them given Trump's progress, while others have used LawFare. For example, one exiled immigrant who has been here eleven years with a battered wife and family has been registered as a member of M-13 by at least two judges. It would appear from the Democratic Party's actions that they do not want to repatriate any of the illegal immigrants, as they represent liberal votes.

Artificial Intelligence (AI)

A concerning aspect of our foreign policy is the competition with China over AI, which is rapidly eroding our lead and enabling China to gain control of autonomous AI and its applications. One expert indicates that by 2030, AI will be autonomous, self-generating, and capable only of making what it determines to be the 'right' decisions—neither good nor bad, just optimal. As we pursue the AI path, several legislative and global considerations must be taken into account. Will we be able to take the lead and fully control AI activities by 2030, especially in the face of competition from China? Does the Defense Department recognize the weak position we would be in if China controlled AI by 2030? And what kind of defenses could we develop against a dominating AI that resists any U.S. controls?

This is a serious consideration for the technology of the free world. Chinese dominance in AI could clearly affect future generations.

If China controls AI, we may not have to fear invasion, because AI agents could overcome and snuff us out in a few seconds. So it's going to be a tough race. Can the slight edge we now have over other countries be sustained? If not, China will have de facto political and economic control of the world. And can we survive the embargoes China has imposed on the use of rare-earth and strategic materials worldwide?

Taxes

I believe pursuing tariffs before making the 2017 tax cuts permanent was a mistake, but, of course, that's hindsight in 2020.

The American people are not forensic accountants; they see what they see today and draw their own conclusions. Meanwhile, government budgeting is largely constrained by the CBO, which, unfortunately, ignores dynamic accounting forecasting and instead focuses solely on historical data. Therefore, CBO accounting, which ignores any positive results from cutting taxes, as the "Big, Beautiful Bill" proposes, overlooks future activity that will significantly reduce the national debt. So far, they have seen little or no abatement in inflation, nor any improvement in the cost of living. And, as we have been told again and again, kitchen-table economics are key here. Also, timing.

The Democrats, who don't want to see advances for our country under Trump's second presidency, are trying to jam everything he's trying to do. They encourage CBO accounting, which projects only the cost of some bills, not their true effect. Yes, tariffs will yield huge benefits (I hope), but these will be subtle to the average American voter. What the average American voter will recognize is a lower cost of living, lower tax payments, and greater harmony worldwide.

Trump embarked on these objectives on January 20, 2025, and I believe (eventually) they will come to pass, but right now it seems doubtful they will happen in time for the midterms, where, based on today's favorable trends, the president and his party could take a further hit, disempowering him from making the inroads he desires and the people should want. I have to say it's almost amazing and un-American that the Democratic Party has apparently suspended providing any meaningful help for the American people and their millions of voters, such as tax reductions, in order to deter the Republicans and their elected leader. Law-Fare from the courts and LIE-WARE from the media enhance Democrats' story, which many people apparently swallow just as they did the "Biden is sharp as a tack" claim for four years.

Just as they believed, "eliminating our energy independence would help push the wrongheaded effort to save America's climate through the Green Lobby, while 'open borders' are claimed to be helping millions and providing labor for farms."

At mid-year 2025, only a small percentage of the fifteen to twenty million illegal immigrants are working on farms. And these farm jobs are probably at the expense of hard-working migrant workers who look forward to legally picking and harvesting crops in the U.S. and then returning to their own country.

I retired from CBS and Fox well before the Trump years, so I was not in any position to arbitrate how the news was presented differently by Fox, CNN, and CBS.

But I know that Fox was more upbeat, more positive, and probably more truthful. They were not above hyping some truths to make a story stronger, but I felt they were largely accurate in their reporting, perhaps because they had a better story to tell and more optimism among their viewers and readers in the recent elections. Democrats who had been led down the primrose path were shocked and deeply depressed when the results were recorded on November 4, 2024. They had been told that the financially challenged Kamala Harris was a shoo-in. They had been so deeply warned or convinced that Trump was a Nazi and that democracy was over as we know it that they felt they had lost their country. In fact, I believe the election results were positive for democracy as Trump tries to right the ship again, as he did in the first term, which apparently went unnoticed by the competing party.

"Trump Derangement Syndrome" became a phrase that accurately described the moods and thoughts of most liberal Democrats, as, according to their networks, social media, magazines, and newspapers, reporting that "America has been dead and buried," brought down by a cabal of the rich who allegedly are trying to enslave our middle and lower classes to increase their wealth and power.

Regarding 'soaking the rich,' in 2022, the top five percent paid sixty-one percent of income tax revenue while earning just over a third of reported income.

The Democrats, and in fact, no one has specified what the rich's fair share should be. They just criticize and leave it hanging to rally their jealous voters.

Punish the rich who are the instigators and supporters of new technologies, new businesses, and new companies and who have been largely responsible for this country's financial growth, including:

AI, supercomputers, social media, communications, and entertainment technologies. There's no way to know what the future holds, but unless we secure a dominant position over China in AI by 2030, China will control us, and eventually our so-called "free people" will be subservient to Chinese dominance.

Government Defense

Our success depends on maintaining a superpower-level budget. Our defense budget has been anemic at best, with little foresight into possible battles, skirmishes, or wars, but is expected to rise in 2025 to at least $900 billion, equal to the interest we pay on our $36 trillion federal debt.

We also continue to order and reorder the same inadequate military equipment we used in the 1960s. Hopefully, with this new budget, we will be able to update our purchases to better support a stronger defense, possibly including a defensive dome over strategic pathways. We should also move aggressively into AI and complete programs that address emerging threats. There are reports and concerns that Russia is developing a nuclear-powered anti-satellite system (ASAT) that could, at the push of a button, disrupt U.S. communications, navigation, and banking. It is not yet designed to eliminate all of our energy infrastructure, but the potential for doing so exists. The reports suggest that a nuclear-powered ASAT could disable or destroy satellites, and crucial communication services do exist now, but not specifically a weapon designed to eliminate all energy.

Reaction to Trump's tax reduction is just beginning to be felt in the spring of 2026.

Advice to Democrats

Try to be happy about the state of the country. Since we Republicans tolerated Biden for four years, whose administration was led by elements that don't like us and are trying to set back the United States for decades, it's hard to be happy. Apparently, for China, everything Joe tried to do far better served the Chinese than the Americans. The reaction to Trump's tax reductions is just beginning to be felt in the spring of 2026 and could help in the midterms.

Global Warming

First, Democrats should resign themselves to Trump being in power for almost three more years. Admittedly, he is trying to unwind several of Biden's actions, such as allowing immigrants into this country, reducing our global energy dominance to focus on green renewable power, and continuing the excess spending that characterized the Democratic years.

Democrats, try to understand how your party accommodated the decline of our energy dominance and adopted the theory that pollution could be reversed, saving the world from an inevitable heat wave and intolerable global warming. Good intentions, bad science.

I remember when Newsweek magazine's cover story in the 1970s claimed that we had to worry about Global Cooling, in which low temperatures would render us helpless and eventually eradicate the United States and most of the frozen world by the turn of the 20th century.

I also read that, due to global warming, Ohio would become an ocean state by 2020, with rising tides. Yet here we are, still recklessly rushing toward temperature oblivion. We now know that fossil fuels are needed to power solar or windmills. We realized that if we had been more aggressive in pursuing nuclear energy and Liquid Natural Gas (LNG), we would be further along in cleaning the atmosphere than we are now. However, I think the panic has somewhat abated as air quality has slightly improved.

The perception of Biden, his mental acuity, and his tragic struggle with prostate cancer that has spread to his bones is a reality the United States may not overcome for years.

This was done and locked up most of the mainstream media who misled millions of Americans in voting for Kamala Harris, which would have heralded a further degeneration of our country. The combination of these two factors – the White House's control of Biden, plus a complicity by a deranged media – could easily have permanently damaged our country if it had not already done so. As said in the previous chapter, we have totally underestimated the cost and the political price of the Biden administration.

We have reiterated that the specific manipulation of Biden and the state he has unwittingly maintained has infected our immigration policy, energy policy, military buildup, foreign policy, and economy. I believe the anger is just now beginning to build among the Republicans and should be shared by the Democrats who have been hoodwinked by this poisonous cabal, promoted by the media. We all should be angry.

Innocent Democratic Party voters were misled, as their officials (mostly unelected) lied about Biden's competence and assured them that Kamala Harris was the rightful elected leader.

Meanwhile, Republicans have been stunned by the unverified information after the election. Although most of us who tune into the news cannot help but conclude that something was amiss with Biden's mental acuity, I thought that if this were true, he would have been removed from the presidency and subsequently barred from participating in the 2024 election.

Democrats, depending on your level of anger, should now push your elected officials to reform the party, remove the far-left think tanks that fostered this, and put forward respectable, intelligent candidates in the future. Without this, I fear Democrats will suffer most in the general elections and further undermine the two-party system, which I believe in, as it has served the United States for more than a century and has kept the other party honest, generally leading to the best outcomes. Forget about the Trump derangement syndrome and start looking for positive features in your current president. I know your objectivity about this man has been poisoned, but we Republicans have been heartened by his election, as Biden's moves were disastrous (perhaps unwittingly) and clearly contrary to the interests of all Americans. We will not resolve the damage the last presidency has brought upon this nation soon, but Democrats, with your help, we can set things right and proceed toward what should be the most exciting Century ever, as we face positive news in medicine, science, technology, supercomputers, and space travel.

I believe that in the coming decades we will experience a tremendous surge in the United States' prospects, including welfare, finance, the human condition, our health, our medicine, and the foreseeable probability of having a truly worldwide, equitable trading system, which will further benefit our international relations with our trading partners, if not the world.

As I mentioned earlier, Mr. Trump clearly has some unlikable traits. He is sometimes boisterous and overbearing, but these are also signs of a clear, forceful leader. He has been a playboy (which many men might have been as well if they had billions and all sorts of women pursuing them). Now he seems to be improving his image and receiving worldwide admiration. The key now is not to let his ego get in the way of progress, which, so far, he has been pretty levelheaded about. He might still appear overly aggressive and capable of initiating some risky programs, such as tariffs, but he is also a keen strategist, and I believe he has had four years out of office to think through the nation's problems and, in a surge of tremendous enthusiasm, is pushing this country in a new and better direction.

I know his actions have mock-terrified the left-wing media, but they are also looking for any misstep on his part or any statement they can criticize until they're proven wrong. I know that not all my readers will share my conservative views. But I hope they will share some of them and become more pragmatic.

Take some time to read the other party's press, and I advise this for both Democrats and Republicans.

I also pray that my Democratic friends evolve out of their dorms and realize that perhaps a country is not being run by a crazy Nazi but someone who has the potential to be the best president ever if he doesn't go off half-cocked. Think about the love in the world: a love that exists not just among humans but throughout much of the natural world—even among wildlife and within the oceans.

Be positive about the future, because it will unfold, and you will see, as I hope, that we are improving every day, and believe some of the benefits of the first Trump administration (which the mainstream media has largely withheld from you), but teemed with truth, they were largely very impressive results.

I firmly believe that the American people will help us emerge from the damage done and that there will be a clear road ahead for prosperity, peace, and Goodwill on Earth.

Scott Bessent said, "Gavin Newsome may be the only Californian who knows less than Kamala Harris."

New Technology

2025 was the year of "Quantum Science and Technology."

Among other new technologies, AI stands out as the most promising for our future. This, combined with the capabilities of the Quantum Computer, will demonstrably change our lives, and we are in a critical race with China for supremacy in this field. The Chinese have developed a costly "quantum supremacy" computer, which they claim is "one quadrillion times faster than the best supercomputers on the planet." Quantum computers can be a tremendous help in medicine, as complete body diagnoses can be done in seconds. At the same time, the computers can read all of a human's blood components and individual organ functions and, eventually, be able to do a complete, actionable diagnosis of an individual's needs and cures.

Medical research can soon do in minutes, if not seconds, what would take ten to fifty years of traditional research by testing and eliminating every possibility as it seeks the correct solution. The longevity of humans born today could exceed 110 years. In twenty-five years, it will not be a total rarity to have individuals 125-140 years or older roaming the Earth.

While these services may appear to add to the already high medical costs for the aging, the ability to diagnose and recommend new medical technologies should greatly reduce costs and eliminate misdiagnoses.

In seconds, we can not only pinpoint cures but deliver them for far less cost. Very early diagnosis will become a factor in building longer, healthier lives and avoiding very expensive costs.

Most technologies will also benefit from the Quantum Era, as various solutions will be developed to improve and extend life, primarily through early diagnosis and targeted treatments. "This is truly the wonderful, healthy world of tomorrow."

However, history has shown that technological breakthroughs are a 'double-edged sword' that can both improve and harm the human condition. But at the same time, produce weapons of mass instruction more easily and quickly. Without doubt, AI and Quantum Computing will have immeasurable effects on our lives and possibly on our deaths.

It is ironic to me that now the Democratic minority party is trying to hold up Trump's "Big Beautiful Bill," which has been designed to help the people and is for lowering taxes on overtime, tips, and wages. A negative vote would instead have led to an average 58% increase across the board in taxes.

I mentioned that the Democratic Party was once the party of the people, but is now "the party against the people" as they are so far refusing *to* vote for lower taxes, deporting illegal immigrants, providing tax relief on tips and overtime, and are simply playing a game of denying anything Trump wants despite its benefit for the American people.

It's almost as if they inherited Biden's mind warp and formed an anti-Trump party.

Iran War With Israel

Surah 2:191: "And kill them (non-Muslims) wherever you find them…kill them. Such is the recompense of the disbelievers (non-Muslims)."

It's hard to believe that Iranians, and for that matter, all Muslims, believe that non-believers should be killed. They also believe that if you are killed while fighting non-Muslims, you have a good shot at heaven. These points should be taken into account when analyzing the Iran-Israel conflict.

Although Iran knows it is overpowered by Israel, in its quest to develop a nuclear bomb and kill Israelis, it has launched a long-range war, using all sorts of devastating projectiles against the country (Israel), which has a better army, nuclear weapons, and strong associations with non-Muslim countries, including the U.S., which recently took out Iran's nuclear weapons program.

Perhaps in the near future, Iran will be overthrown by its suffering people and once again become a prosperous trading ally to the U.S. and the world, not under a religious totalitarian leadership, but closer to a democratic country run for and by its people.

Trump's successful cultivation of Middle Eastern alliances in 2025 only strengthens his voice and underscores his ultimatums.

No Kings

It is fascinating that crowds of liberal demonstrators have openly come out against "Kings." Our country has resisted kingship for 250 years, beginning with George Washington, who famously declined a crown. The United States, regardless of party, has rejected the idea of ever moving to a king. In the UK, with today's access to the happenings of their royal families, we've had more of an inside look at the advantages and disadvantages of having a king. I doubt that people in Henry VIII's time had any real insight into his personality, given the backdrop of the Church's unrest over his desire for a divorce. Since then, we've been very observant of the benefits and drawbacks of having kings in this day and age, who serve more as symbolic figures than rulers. We have also observed some scandals and infighting, which have been set up to portray the Royal family as real people, with jealousy, pain, and family struggles.

Donald Trump, who is hated and dismissed by half of Congress, can't be called a King.

Democrats' Reaction To The B.B.B

To paraphrase the Wall Street Journal (July 5, 2025) opinion piece titled "No One is 'Gutting' the Safety Net."

Democrats, together with their bedfellow, the liberal media, distort GOP policy, but their coverage of the Beautiful Big Bill has hit a new low.

The WSJ goes on to say, "Allow us to temper the histrionics about gutting the social safety net with a few facts about Medicaid, food stamps, and Republican priorities."

The Wall Street points out that the accusations of the Democrats are that the new Republican Big Bill "will toss millions from Medicaid and cut the program to the bone."

They go on to say that "Democrats have offered cynical distortions, including pregnant women in poverty and disabled children will suffer."

CBO has claimed at least 4.8 million won't comply with the Bill's part-time work requirement, and they go on to say that the working poor will be lost in red tape as they try to prove they're 'on the job'."

States have handled work requirements in food, stamps, and cash assistance for decades.

Also, the millions they are "throwing off the bill" are younger single individuals with no young children who are currently not working but drawing liberally on Medicaid and Medicare. They are given thirty days to find a job for only twenty hours a week. This, I believe, will not only boost their self-esteem but also increase the number of workers, raising the employment rate and helping the economy.

The Journal continues: "Democrats think they can ride the Medicaid scare to a midterm victory, but there's still time for the GOP to present the facts."

And this, I believe, is the battle we Republicans have foreseen for a number of years, in which we have to stop the Democratic media from misinforming their party and their voters for years through Lie-Ware and other tactics.

The Bamboozling of Democratic Voters

Most of you probably don't know what has happened to your party. How they've been maneuvered and, in turn, have maneuvered you in the wrong direction. Traditionally, Democrats have been negative about world affairs and consider themselves victims, making dour predictions about their country's ruination. Sound familiar?

They believe the real enemy is Donald Trump. For years, the New York Times, the Washington Post, and other left-wing media have attacked and vilified him in every possible way. If there is no political balance in your life, it's because you have not sought out other points of view, philosophies, and information about our country's strategies. Every act Trump performs and everything he says are subject to angry criticism by your party. I have listed the wrong positions liberals have taken elsewhere in the book, but Republicans have viewed Democrats as miserable, gloomy people. They have less hope, less balance, and less spiritual support in their lives, and victimization has become a buzzword. I'm sure my simple book has angered you, but before you completely dismiss it, let me suggest that you at least consider another point of view and allocate perhaps 10% of your reading/viewing time to alternative perspectives. This may involve watching the dreaded FOX, in which case I might suggest spending a few minutes with Jesse Watters or Larry Kudlow, who offer a more optimistic view of America's prospects going forward. After that, you may shake your head at the preposterous claims you hear from fellow Democrats, but if you had the luxury of looking back for a year or so, you would see that most of their prognostications about the Right, financial forecasts, and proposed Acts have held up. If you'd like to read, you may also look at Newsmax magazine or view their free app, Newsmax TV. Maybe you won't agree with anything you hear at first, but as situations unfold, you may find they are more accurate than the gloomy, dread-filled CNN, MSNBC, and CNBC, all of whom missed out on the Biden debacle. While you are reading the New York Times, the Washington Post, or other left-wing publications, you might also tune in to the Wall Street Journal's opinion page or editorials. This may be painful for you, but I suspect you would be a happier, more confident person regarding your current government than you have been in the last few years. Try it!

It is very frustrating for the author and the Republican Party to deal with a liberal party that does not understand how Trump will benefit the country. Almost everything he wants to do will benefit our democracy and the people. For example, they are against the big, beautiful bill, which your party calls the Big Ugly Bill.

- Permanently reducing tax rates.
- A 4 to 6% increase in GDP
- Helps reduce the national debt.
- No tax on tips.
- No tax on overtime
- No tax on Social Security
- Full factory expensing of P&E
- Pave the way to a golden future.

While the Democratic Party in Congress has sat and will sit on their hands during this critical vote, they are more concerned with politics and themselves than with this great country's future and welfare.

Please read summaries of the Big Beautiful Bill plan and start listening to a little bit of positive news from more conservative outlets. Understand that the health plan hoax kept our country closed for a month.

If you do, you will be happier in the future, less depressed by your party's negativity and lack of progress, and you will enjoy our booming new economy.

And save some admiration for your president, who was able to eviscerate Iran's nuclear systems without waging war. The Iranians may respond with retaliatory measures.

Difference in Party Attitudes

The last Gallup poll I would like to show reflects the percentage of people satisfied with the way things are going in the United States:

Democrats 1% Satisfied
Republicans 76% Satisfied
Independents 23% Satisfied

Although the rise in crime is a factor in these poll numbers, this once again signals to me that the Democratic base really does not know what's going on in the country and that they have been muzzled, blinded, and lied to about what has taken place. They are focused on ICE as an incursion rather than recognizing it as an effort to round up undocumented immigrants.

As I explained, following the tactical bombing of Iran, as you might expect, Congressional Democrats immediately complained that they were not counseled on this move. Suppose the Democratic Congress had known the specifics of the attack. In that case, I am sure that the far-left members of this body would have leaked it to the press, which obviously would've endangered our bomber pilots, our troops, and military installations.

Once again, the Democrats are calling for the president's impeachment, claiming he violated the rules of war in Iran. Will they ever get on board? I recognize that their foreign policy amounts to nothing more than appeasement, a naïve concept in the modern world. Undoubtedly, all we will hear from the left-wing media will be about Trump's warmongering. Instead of recognizing the strategy and precision the president used to avoid all-out war, "denying the world of an enemy with devastating nuclear capability," they will continue to criticize.

They also don't seem to realize that a precision strike on Iran's nuclear activity, rather than on the country, could save many lives in the Middle East and possibly protect our troops stationed in the region.

BOOK TWO

Chapter 9 | 2026 OUTLOOK

As Plato warned in the 4th century B.C, *"One of the penalties of refusing to participate in politics is that you end up being governed by your inferiors."*

Obviously, in the next year, there will be both setbacks and positive outcomes. Areas I suspect will flare up.

The Economy

Most experts are proposing an excellent financial picture for the United States and the world in 2026. This will happen if several things fall into place:

1. War in Iran successfully ends.
2. Fed interest rates continue to come down.
3. Tariffs produce positive cash flow and help improve U.S. international relations.
4. Energy opportunities have opened, and such practices as exploration, new wells, fracking, and rapid development of nuclear energy take place.
5. Trump's tax incentives to foreign investors for building plants and equipment in the US are successful.
6. Maintenance of original (pre-COVID) tax policies.
7. Reform of taxes on tips and 'overtime.'
8. Successful attempts to eliminate nonproductive illegal aliens from our shores.
9. Crime abatement progresses.

10. AI helps build a productive U.S. labor force without recession or high unemployment.
11. Our adversaries, China and Russia, do not take aggressive or provocative steps toward war.
12. Republicans keep control of both houses of Congress at midterms.
13. URE becomes a reality. Rare Earths.
14. Robot domination continues in the U.S.

There should be a thorough investigation into who controlled the Autopen and who has helped undermine our country through the devastating and ruinous decisions of the Biden years. This should not be ignored, as it is not merely a historical fact but a warning to our national stability and future protections.

The Future of Media

Two Factors That Will Affect Media Balance in the Future

Factor One - The Media

Encourage right-wing media to expand, especially as the Fox Empire could start sliding towards the left. Hint: A right-wing group of investors could possibly take over Fox in the next two years to prevent slippage and continue their mission. There will never be completely sanitized news media, but a television program that covers truth and lies each week could help level the playing field and bring some semblance of truth arbitration to listeners.

This "Truth or Lies" venture would have to be programming set apart from right or left-wing media, self-standing and monitored by a permanent group of three Democrats and three Republicans. I note that Fox has settled its disturbing legal battle with Rupert's least liberal offspring, Lachlan Murdoch, who survives as CEO of both FOX Corp. and News Corp. Cash was used as an offset to the non-controlling heirs.

Recently, CBS appointed an ombudsman to monitor bias. Kenneth Weinstein, formerly the CEO of the Hudson Institute (a right-wing organization), will earn $250,000 per year for just one day of work each month, in part to offset the network's Democratic political slant. This is a good first step, but Mr. Weinstein will still report to CBS's parent, Paramount Skydance, which, for the first time, will be in the "Republican" hands of Larry Ellison and his son.

Factor Two - Larry Ellison

The pendulum, favoring left-wing media, may swing toward a more balanced political landscape than ever before. To date, FOX properties have held the lone position on conservative values, and now could have company via Larry Ellison, founder of Oracle, who recently and briefly became the richest man in the world, momentarily surpassing Musk. Larry has aggressively moved into film and TV. Together with his son, David Ellison, CEO of Skydance Media, he has recently become the owner of Paramount (including CBS). I also understand that Larry has made a successful offer for Warner: Discovery and its properties, which could include CNN and HBO. If so, we would start to see a more balanced mix between Democratic- and Republican-linked media.

If he is successful, this could be a major shift in the Republican Party's political influence. Ellison has been a key Trump supporter and helped bankroll the president's campaign, so he will likely be influential in seeing media under his control shift to the right, providing more conservative reporting. In the long run, this could open the eyes of both Republicans and Democrats, as the overall news will become more conservative and truthful.

Crime

Almost everybody in the United States is fed up with record levels of crime, particularly in major blue cities. Trump has tried to rein in crime, notably in DC, and is threatening other blue cities where crime levels are frankly intolerable. Incredibly, the leaders of sanctuary cities and states where crime is rampant are screaming against any possibility of Trump coming to their apparently unwanted aid to wipe crime from their streets. These mayors and governors in sanctuary cities and states appear both rigid and determined that they need no help, and ironically threaten to battle troops sent by the White House in their streets. O'er the ramparts!

"Socialism is fine until you run out of other people's money."

- Margaret Thatcher

New York City

In 2026, New York has a socialist-communist mayor. To me, that sounds like a death knell for New York City unless Mamdani is stopped. He appears to favor several insidious approaches to governing the world's largest financial center. According to Raphael A. Mangual, Mamdani has made pledges:

- The full elimination of cash bail, taking the current state's disastrous bail reform even further.
- Outright decriminalization of drug possession and prostitution.
- Eliminating mandatory minimum sentences
- Retroactively lowering all maximum sentences.
- Fighting the construction of the Borough-based jails meant to replace the soon-to-be-closed Rikers Island.

Taken together, these proposals amount to a repudiation of police effectiveness and funding, thereby complicating efforts to reduce crime and to address policy in New York City.

This goes beyond "defund the police." It would effectively handicap law enforcement and risk undermining public order. The prospects for my birth city look bleak under Mamdani, and it is hard to imagine New Yorkers knowingly electing a crisis-prone administration. Martial law could be considered in extreme circumstances if future events warranted it.

WARNING! While trying to solve the mystery of why Mamdani is apparently a shoo-in for Mayor of

New York City, I discovered that most of his city voters were born in other countries. They have come here for various reasons, but I assume that most did not grow up with a typical American ethos or family structure, received different schooling, and never had to learn the basics of democracy. This is not only a warning of problems to come in our largest city, but it will also influence other major cities, especially sanctuary cities, where non-Americans and criminals could sway the vote. This could lead to major issues in future elections, especially if the Democratic Party promotes and supports these non-American-born individuals.

Is this xenophobia? No, it's the survival of democracy.

Defund the Police

With New York City already a sanctuary city and its motto of "defund the police," can you imagine the chaos, crime, and death that will result from Mamdani's policies? It may come down to Trump dealing with this man as an individual, fostering Socio-Communism, who has been elected to run our largest city into the ground.

Again, Democrats will hurl invective against Trump, the "Nazi president."

Youth & Charlie Kirk

Here are three respected quotes about Youth.

1. "Our youth now love luxury; they have bad manners and contempt for authority; they show

disrespect for elders and prefer chatter to exercise. Children are now tyrants."

2. "What is happening to our young people? They disrespect their elders and disobey their parents. They ignore the law and riot in the streets."
3. "The world is passing through troublous times. Young people today often think only of themselves. They have no reverence for parents or for old age. They are impatient with all restraint. They talk as if they knew everything, and what passes for wisdom among us is foolishness to them. As for the girls, they are forward, immodest, and unladylike in speech, behavior, and dress."

The fact that these quotes from Plato and Socrates are nearly 3000 years old suggests that youth has been a perturbing state for mature individuals. Many of the great philosophers' views on children could be applied today.

Why are we losing our children to good sense? And in many cases, to the disparagement of their government and even assassination, as in the case of Charlie Kirk.

My family had a motto that I think Charlie would have aspired to: "Post Tenebras Speramus, Lux et De Lumine."

Or "after the darkness we look for the light of lights." I think Charlie would have agreed with this aphorism, and most of us are sure that Charlie now dwells with the light of lights. He was an effective answer for young people today, who are quite a bit at sea. Instinctively, he knew that speaking and preaching alone would be ineffective, so he sought out conversations and peaceful discussions of differences. The youth have largely responded to this unique form of debate and to Charlie.

Today's youth are largely mesmerized by social media and hate speech, and their lack of historical knowledge leads them to make flat statements and respond angrily. They frequently lack knowledge of the democratic process and the American way.

Charlie also emphasized the importance of a belief greater than yourself as a factor in self-reliance and self-worth. I have mentioned that one part of the Democratic Party mindset is a lack of belief in anything outside ourselves, a sense of being alone in this complex world, alone to fight the setbacks and dilemmas we all face.

We, 21st-century people, think we are uniquely beset by troubles such as drug use, screen addiction, poor grades, lies spread by social media, brainwashing, and material values. Our youth are not only vastly important to the young but also to all of us, our future, our children, and our politics.

I must single out Charlie Kirk as a man who sought to instill in our youth positive thinking, prayer, and a sense of Christ's outstretched arms. He welcomed debate, discussion, and differences of opinion. Rather than preaching and teaching, he engaged in discussion. He effectively promoted faith among our younger citizens. He sought to counter the negative thinking of our youth, who were being poisoned by irresponsible media, by linking Christian principles to their lives and instilling self-respect. Like Jesus, this man died in his early thirties, but both left a lasting impact on mankind. In his unique way of engaging youth, he avoided preaching, sermons, and righteousness, favoring discussion and conversation as a touchstone. Just days after his death, we saw that approximately 124,000 new groups had come forward, seeking to set up their own Turning Point clubs.

The outright negativity following Charlie's death has fueled violence and hate, which should be muzzled. In fact, Vice President J.D. Vance and White House Deputy Chief of Staff Steven Miller told the NY Post in October '25 that they were working on an "organized strategy to go after left-wing organizations that are promoting violence" in the wake of Charlie's assassination.

As a first step, I think the US has to take control of social media, such as TikTok, which exploits our youth and provides personal data to China.

Trump Outlook 2026

For knowledgeable Republicans, Trump has generally managed most domestic and foreign issues very well. The one overarching criticism, despite an otherwise stellar performance, is his egocentrism. His proposed naming of a D.C. stadium and the Kennedy Center after himself, as well as other roads, boulevards, and justice complexes he influenced, may not sit well with many. He now declares that the $300 million White House ballroom will not be named after him, but many regard this as outrageous, ego-driven spending, even though it doesn't use taxpayer money. The sale of an increasing number of products under his name, including everything from two-dollar bills to watches, doesn't improve his image.

A good number of Democrats have loyally adhered to the LieWare messaging of left-wing media, and neither do nor ever will see Trump in a positive light. Democrats, especially women, have heard the vilification of his name for decades from the New York Times and other left-wing media. Trump Derangement Syndrome still exists, and criticism of the man and his personality is constantly demonized in every possible way.

He probably deserves to have a few government structures named after him, but obviously, this is done tastefully posthumously, as with Reagan National Airport. Many take offense, or at least look askance, in varying degrees at the Trump Organization's sales of Trump-named products, including cologne, sneakers, Bibles, dancing ornaments, MAGA hats, toys, talking figures, T-shirts, fake $ 1,000 bills, and real $2 bills.

The dislike for Donald Trump is so deep that a significant shift in opinion among the majority of the seventy-five million who voted against him is unlikely, regardless of what Trump's accomplishments are. We heard more than one commentator say, "If Trump conquered cancer, deeply brainwashed Democrats would still abhor the man." However, it is clear that if the President takes a little more modest approach to most of his accomplishments, the positive impact of some of his decisions, and if he shows just an iota of humility in 2026 and beyond, he would be better served, and so would the G.O.P., for the midterms.

Mr. President, forget personal aggrandizement,

stop exploiting the mercantile advantages of the office, and tone down your name-calling.

Midterms

Trump has improved relations with over 600 countries, cleansing and restoring our country after the disastrous effects of the previous administration, and has provided an incredible vista for the future with lower interest rates, job growth, and a clear point of view on the technology that faces us in the coming years, particularly AI.

Based on these factors, Trump and the Republican Party should be declared the winners in November, as a reward for these achievements. However, it will be the Democrats' effort to sabotage every act that Trump has put in place. Every move he has made, including lowering taxes for our working class. They are also "helping" by closing the government at a time when we should be at our peak to complete the Iran "War."

What Trump has done can largely be undone overnight by the Democrats if they control both houses after the midterms, and our president will, ironically, face certain impeachment for many of the positive things he has achieved. It is clear that the Democrats desperately want to take back Congress and will be largely assisted in this effort by the liberal media, which still dominates the news today.

This would be a serious setback for the United States and our future, as their goals can be achieved only through the prodigious use of Lie-Ware by the Liberal press for the rest of 2026.

It is clear that lifelong Democrats have subjected themselves to and believed the stories generated by this partisan press and are largely unaware of the true story.

If they can render the most successful President in our lifetime (if not in all of history) somewhat powerless by revoking his actions and accomplishments, the US and the World will suffer accordingly over the long term.

Also, should Democrats win the 2028 election, they will immediately amend, change, or replace policies that Trump has put in place, thereby diluting his valiant effort to improve all aspects of our country.

They will surely pursue his impeachment in court proceedings.

In other words, they will sacrifice America's future just to reduce the effectiveness of our current leader. This is blindsided hate, not just political motivation. If the left wins in either the Mid or in '28:

Will we return to open borders?

Will we eliminate our energy efforts?

Will we promote defunding the police, no I.C.E. raids, or efforts to remove illegal aliens from this country?

Will we revert to the apparent Democratic objection to BBB, thereby imposing a fifty-eight percent increase in federal taxes on our taxpayers?

Will the U.S. return to a policy of appeasement toward foreign nations and act without teeth?

Will we have to submit to a huge deficit built by irresponsible tax-and-spend once again?

If so, we will eventually hand our country over to Chinese control! A bleak conclusion, but...

IRA For Babies

It's interesting to see that the president has authorized $1,000 to be deposited into an IRA-type account for newborns. These funds will be managed by private-market funds and will include ETFs and other instruments to provide broad access to key markets.

These investments are the very ones I mentioned in connection with Social Security improvements that could be made for retirement funds, and to avoid any Social Security shutdown or failure. This is genius and should generate up to $1 million in additional income in retirement, in addition to Social Security. A key factor will be preventing early withdrawals by parents or children.

If these IRA funds are adopted by the general population, I would expect to see the same kind of structure for Social Security as for the baby boomers. If left untouched, these funds could accumulate at an average annual rate of 10%, yielding $1 million at retirement, plus Social Security.

So Trump is right: we have the power to provide every child with or near millionaire status at age 67.

Recent Poll

I am flummoxed by a recent Rasmussen poll in which forty-eight percent indicated that Trump was not doing as good a job as Biden as President.

Who are these people who feel that way? Do they welcome having up to 20 million illegal aliens in our country?

Are they against Trump's tax cuts? Are they against the US being honored by most foreign countries?

Are they against or unaware of the benefits of tariffs, which could generate as much as $1 trillion in savings this year? Are they against the U.S. destruction of Iran's nuclear program? Are they unaware of the traitorous acts by the previous White House? Are they unaware of Biden's mental acuity and general health problems?

Or are they so opposed to the US repatriation of illegal aliens that they blame President Trump for efforts to remove these dangerous undocumented individuals from the country? Or are they products of the widespread liberal press, which constantly criticizes President Trump? My main concern for the US is that a large part of the country does not know what is really happening or what actions the current White House has taken. They are either completely unaware of the news or they mostly rely on a Democratic media, which is so warped that it prevents them from exercising good judgment.

In sum, I feel our country will be in good physical shape. Obviously, if any element of the Democratic Party retakes Congress, the task will be much tougher. In recent years, the Democratic Party has clearly proved that it is no longer the party of the people and will probably try to hamstring everything Trump attempts. If they have a majority in either the House or the Senate, we will see. We can only pray that, in the next few years, the government is in the hands of the Republicans while the Democrats are still sitting on their hands when it comes to progress. My fear is the extent to which they can unravel the good bills, acts, tariffs, and appointments that Trump has made, either after the midterms or during the 2028 election.

Hopefully, enlightened Americans will recognize America's potential under Trump and survive. There is also hope that the Democratic Party will return to being a Party of the People—not of the politicians.

Once again, it promotes programs for economic growth and is not mired in Trump Derangement Syndrome.

What Americans should be watching in 2026.

As the nation moves into 2026, every concerned American should stay alert to key developments. Some are expected, while others could catch us off guard. Nonetheless, all will influence the country's future.

1. The economy and the Federal Reserve's inflation, interest rates, and monetary policy will continue to challenge both investors and households.
2. China's empty promises - Watch for unfulfilled trade and diplomatic commitments and observe how the U.S. responds. Plus, even more sorties in the South China Sea and around Taiwan.
3. Artificial Intelligence and Rare Earths - Advances in AI and the management of rare earth materials could shape the next phase of global competition.
4. Is New York's status as the world's financial capital secure, or is it at risk of ideological control?
5. California's tax exodus, driven by high taxes and regulations, is pushing residents and businesses to move elsewhere. Will the trend accelerate?
6. Governor Newsom's Presidential Ambitions. Can a candidate from a troubled state win on the basis of a failed state at the national stage?
7. Mideast unrest—ongoing volatility involving Hamas, Palestine, and Iran could reshape regional alliances.
8. Repatriation of Undocumented Aliens - Will the federal government make meaningful progress on border control and deportation policy?

9. Sanctuary cities in crisis – once symbols of compassion, many are now grappling with rising crime and disorder in public.
10. Energy and Exports – NATO allies and India are seeking reliable partners. Will the U.S. lead or fall behind?
11. Ukraine and Russia – The prolonged conflict continues to drain Russia's economy, but what is the global toll?
12. Media consultation – Ongoing efforts to merge or "level" outlets such as Paramount and CBS raise questions about control and bias.
13. Midterm Elections - Can the GOP retain control of Congress, and what changes might follow?
14. Tariff Policy – Will tariffs finally protect U.S. industries without causing new inflation?
15. The Unforeseen – History shows that what transforms a nation most is what no one predicted.

Rare Earths

Recent developments in the US involve the topic of "rare earths." First, a multi-million-dollar alliance has been established with Brazil and Canada to support the research and development of rare earths and energy metals, in collaboration with the International Development Finance Corporation (DFC). This is a first step toward securing the future availability of rare earths and countering China's near-monopoly on these critical elements.

Additionally, Elon Musk recently announced plans to develop what he calls U.R.E.s. These principles are designed for SpaceX and Tesla and eliminate the need for rare-earth materials across all vehicles. They also support SpaceX in developing planetary rockets and potentially planning a mission to Mars later in the decade. This development should not only be a major scientific breakthrough but also lead to significant cost reductions, benefiting future Tesla cars and all vehicles using these engines. Furthermore, Musk's new element(s) will serve as a crucial enabler for new technologies, both on Earth and in interplanetary travel in the near future.

Chapter 10 | Future of Technology

AI and the World

The tech world is moving extremely fast to develop AI and Super AI capabilities across all aspects. This endeavor will advance AI to the point where it can determine facts and figures without error. In addition to diagnosing and treating diseases, it will provide effective guidance and control over manufacturing, production, and marketing. It will be able to accurately and almost instantaneously assemble all information from around the world, available to everyone. According to John Altucher, "No more fake news. No more fake anything. The word 'news' won't exist."

You will simply be able to determine and have access to all the facts dissected from every angle."

Of course, this also means that the media will no longer be able to easily disassemble or shape the news to the satisfaction of a given political party. This, in my opinion, will have a significant positive effect on American citizens, as Lie-Ware could be eliminated from all literature, reporting, social media, and scientific pronouncements. This should also affect how American citizens think when it becomes available in a few years.

However straightforward the news is, or however the word for news might be "data" in the future, I can't help but think that network news media and social media will still find a way to twist the facts in favor of some cause.

"A senator from Delaware running for president had brazenly stolen a speech by a leader of the Welsh Labor Party in the United Kingdom, and when caught, paid the price by humiliatingly dropping out of the 1988 presidential race."

Morning News

I believe 2026 marks the start of a major technological shift that will change all of our lives, and our children's, demonstrably and forever. What is starting now will exceed every major technological breakthrough in the past, including the Steam Engine, Eli Whitney's cotton gin, Edison's discovery of electric light that lit the world, the automobile, the airplane, and all other momentous tech changes back to early man's discovery of fire and the wheel. Yes, we are on the course of discovery and technological breakthroughs that rival those that have changed lives in the past.

Robots

Instead of autonomous robots taking over our lives as our bosses, chiefs, and leaders, we have to determine how close the technology is to achieving humanization, using robots for information.

Then, hopefully, a pre-prepared action plan, ironically developed by robots, could take its place. We might also need to indoctrinate some of the advanced robots to monitor the situation. But I guess we have several years to worry about and fix this one.

The advent of AI into our lives will also create (temporarily, I hope) a number of problems.

The principal problem would be huge layoffs across the industry, government babysitting, clerical, and factory jobs.

I recently spoke with a senior officer at Morgan Stanley, who said that a single AI system handling Books, P&Ls, and annual reports has replaced thirty of their dedicated workers. This problem of replacing and reassigning the large number of workers who will be laid off is, I assume, a problem for the US and the world. This could result in a huge, multimillion-crowd of educated, loyal employees searching for new opportunities, which probably won't exist.

There are several ways to correct this situation, such as:

- Retraining for new responsibilities.
- Creating a huge fund for the discarded loyal employees. This fund could be generated by taxing the companies for their use of AI.
- Together with funds put aside by the companies themselves for relocating valuable employees who have been victims of AI.
- Using incentives for a few companies **NOT to** use AI or robotics in their work, but to retain these humans in their current jobs with the understanding they could be replaced by AI robotics upon retirement.

Problems for all employers in the future.

Once autonomous robots can perform tasks like humans, it may be difficult to control them. This is a huge problem we should be mindful of and, as development progresses, work to put in place a system of controls.

Also, China still looms as a major competitor in AI.

If they proceeded with autonomous AI, it would be difficult to prevent the control of our government or weaponry, our defense, or our way of life.

As stated, every new scientific breakthrough has brought both benefits for humanity and serious perils, such as nuclear.

AI robotics will be no different.

Giga Plant Texas

As noted, Musk has developed what he calls UREs, which seemingly eliminate the need for rare earths in car assembly and future engines. If true, this could be a major breakthrough for automotive technology and help reduce competition over rare-earth materials with China. One goal of the huge trillion-dollar-and-a-half-dollar IPO and merger is to complete a Giga plant he is building for Tesla in Texas. This plant can apparently produce robotically assembled cars using no rare earths or labor, reportedly for $7,800. He will also be producing millions of AI humanoid robots, as they will be essential across all aspects of life, work, and entertainment, and are expected to be quickly adopted across various sectors. Robots alone represent a trillion-dollar market opportunity on Earth.

DCs in Space

What does Elon Musk plan to accomplish with this new super IPO? His major purpose is the ability for us to establish distribution centers in space which could provide the power needed not only for DCs on earth but future travel to Mars initially by advanced AI robots who can be transported without the extra expense of clothes, food, bathrooms entertainment, Musk has said that because of huge demands of DCs on earth, our planet will run out of electricity in approximately thirty six months for these purposes. By building power-generating space stations, they will not only provide us with power on Earth but also lay the groundwork for terraforming and eventual colonization of Mars, initially by robots, perhaps someday by humans. The red planet provides vast resources that could be mined and used here on Earth.

Mega IPO

Trump, Musk, SpaceX (now merged with AI), Tesla, and Invidia are planning an announcement soon (2026?), which will discuss a massive new merger and IPO. In fact, it is expected to be the largest IPO ever, estimated at over $1.5 trillion. A key new non-rare-earth technology will be covered, and the IPO will announce revolutionary non-rare-earth engines for automotive and robotics as part of the triple merger's objectives. The main objective, however, is to create extraterrestrial data centers. I suspect the combined company will have a tremendous impact on the future, as it will involve a giga-plant for Tesla, possibly the largest in the world, which, according to Musk, will allegedly be able to sell cars for $7,800 due to the elimination of rare-earth magnets and labor in Tesla engines. Also, hundreds of thousands of humanoid robots will be produced to service plants, home offices, and just about every aspect of life you can think of. These robots will not yet be autonomous or capable of thinking/acting like humans, but will be able to replicate basic activities across companies, factories, housewives, farms, industries, and defense development. One key role for them will be space exploration (hence SpaceX), relieving humans of years of travel and the costs of human conveniences, such as air, bathrooms, sleeping accommodations, food, and entertainment. These forays into space will allow mapping the surface of Mars, terraforming the planet for future mining, and beaming the info back to Earth.

When robots reach autonomy, they will expand into all areas of our lives, including management, construction, research, and education, and, in fact, into any simple or complex function humans will require in the future. The details of this forthcoming merger/IPO are not yet well known, but its purpose should represent a dramatic improvement in our lives in the very near future.

It will be important that these future robots remain under human control, thus preventing a drastic future 'Civil War' when they attain full autonomy; otherwise, our roles could be reversed, and we could become their slaves.

A quote from Musk

"Electric power to push AI forward won't be available on Earth at any price in approximately 36 months." Marrying space rocket and AI companies will help provide incremental power, as the cheapest place to source the necessary power will be in space, where data centers will generate more power than Earthbound data centers can now provide. A "huge undertaking," perhaps fraught with unforeseeable and unimaginable problems.

The biggest threat AI poses today (aside from massive layoffs) is that the large CAPEX required to achieve these lofty and varied AI objectives could leave us both critically cash and credit-poor after the rush into new startups and the subsequent $2.0 trillion-plus in IPOs.

Some restraint is needed here to monitor and control this exuberance.

Iran Attack

Peace in the Middle East. This concept has always seemed unattainable. Now, thirty-five countries have joined Donald Trump in overseeing peace between Hamas and Israel. A noble accomplishment by our president, but we should recognize that peace is very difficult to achieve and probably much harder to maintain.

In other words, it's easier said than done! Our recent attack on Iran illustrates this, showing a populace (Iran) that has been totally suppressed by its arcane leadership, while its plans seem to call for the elimination of Israel, followed by an attack on the

U.S., as a start in their effort to wipe out Democracy wherever it flourishes. Either we take this country on now or wait until they have restored their nuclear capability and are prepared to be a major factor, probably as a key part of World War III. Concerned Americans are already demonstrating in the streets with a hue and cry against sending our troops into battle, forgetting that Iran has long been the major purveyor of terror around the world and is better stopped now, at their weakest point, than after a rebuild of destructive nuclear weaponry in a war in which millions, if not billions, of people will perish.

Again, this illustrates a complete lack of pragmatism, foresight, and judgment on the part of the US demonstrators, who are probably mostly liberal minded and prefer to coddle and defer rather than face the harsh music now.

I also can't conclude that the Democratic Party is in any way patriotic, as they have closed our government during this intense battle for Iran's future.

Iran is known for

A) It's Brutality
B) Mass Repression
C) Human Rights Violator
D) China, Russia Ally
E) World Piracy

China

We, the people, seem to be vaguely aware that China is poised to confront us on several fronts; however, an exhaustive study of China would reveal that its competitiveness extends to every aspect of American life and every organizational activity. We seem to be aware of the COVID-19 pandemic, which some commentators have linked to China's early outbreak; of its military buildup; of accusations that it has acquired foreign technology and intellectual property through a range of means; of its significant control over rare earth elements and other critical materials used for strategic weapons; and of its increasing investment presence in U.S. real estate markets.

However, very few seem to realize that, over the last few decades, the United States has been economically intertwined with China's growth, including sectors that may contribute to its military and technological development, corporate growth, and various acquisitions in the United States (particularly in the heartland and near military bases). There are several culprits here, but one of the key ones is Wall Street, which facilitates investment in Chinese companies. Americans investing in stocks of many important and strategic organizations in China have been a major contributor to China's dominance and growth. China has a dual objective: to acquire Taiwan Semiconductor Manufacturing Company (TSM), the world's largest chipmaker, and to assert control over the South China Sea.

By controlling the South China Sea, they will control shipping and build defenses against any effort to save independent Democratic Taiwan from the clutches of its big red brother. Stopping these investments is very difficult, as our treasury department and other financial institutions are clearly geared toward fostering American investment in Chinese stocks (which have previously disappointed their American investors).

It will be difficult for Trump and his cabinet to wean U.S. investors away from the temporary allure of Chinese financial instruments, and equally challenging for American markets to enforce laws that prohibit hedge funds, mutual funds, ETFs, and other investment vehicles from holding Chinese stocks.

The fact is that the CCP's modus operandi is to encourage foreign investment, including from Americans and others in democracies, in Chinese stocks. In turn, let these investments finance Chinese technology and war preparations (and, in the end, possibly deprive their foreign investors of any recovery of their funds).

It would seem Americans have been unaware of this tricky way to use Americans' money to subsidize Chinese activities, particularly on the military and technological fronts. You would also have to assume that many banks, brokerage firms, and hedge funds are presenting these investment opportunities in ways that critics argue may not fully disclose the associated risks.

On a personal basis, without being fully aware of the intricacies and nuances, I believe President Trump should appoint a new Chinese Affairs Director for a Cabinet-level post who can focus on China's many "wars," including its approach to engineering, its monopoly on Rare Earth resources, and its growing military efforts and political inroads; track its AI technologies; and tighten security around our Intellectual Property. Candidates for this critical office must be able to work effectively with the State, Treasury, and Defense Departments, as well as all U.S. cabinet departments.

Three capable men come to mind for this role.

- Mike Pompeo, former Secretary of State, Director of the CIA, and Captain in the U.S. Army, who graduated first in his class from West Point.
- General Jack Keane, a retired four-star general, seems clearly to visualize the dangers to the United States around the world. He is articulate in summarizing these conditions and possible countermeasures.
- Senator Tom Cotton, who, in my opinion, clearly sees the multi-channeled effort of the Chinese Communist Party to challenge us and "battle" us at every turn, to defeat us on every level now and in the future.

Hopefully, the government will also make the case for a thorough investigation into any potential foreign influence on U.S. policymaking, including concerns about the Biden administration. As noted, China is clearly waging a war against the United States on these many fronts:

- Mastery of Artificial Intelligence
- Warfare/Military Build-Up

- Space
- Farmland in the U.S.
- The ultimate Bomb
- Strategic Rare Earth Materials
- Energy
- U.S. Youth Infiltration through social media
- Spyware
- Taiwan Strait Protection
- Control of oceans/passageways in the South. China Sea
- Intellectual Property/Trade Secrets
- Support Socialist Governments
- Race for AI supremacy

A country that has the goal, the wherewithal, and the power to undermine the U.S.?

Examples:

1. Some theories have suggested that COVID-19 originated from a laboratory in China, which has infected the world and killed more than one million American citizens.

2. As we've just pointed out, Biden's presidential actions largely aligned with Chinese interests, weakening our nation. As President Trump has said, "who would be nuts enough to purposely open our borders" to the world's large numbers of undocumented migrants, estimated at ten to twenty million people. Some of them might become decent American citizens, but some critics

argue that insufficient screening and economic pressures may increase crime-related risks.

3. Besides COVID, China is suspected of recently introducing a fungus, which could eventually destroy our crops and potentially lead to starvation among Americans.

4. There have been numerous allegations and documented cases indicating that Chinese entities have engaged in intellectual property theft, causing untold financial losses and insecurity for the U.S.
5. They have developed advanced war machines that could significantly challenge U.S. capabilities in several scenarios.

6. Due to the steps taken by the previous White House, we have been plunged into energy insufficiency rather than supremacy, and our enemies have been able to supply fossil fuels to NATO members in Europe that were previously supplied by the U.S.

7. There have been ongoing concerns that they have infiltrated our country through scientists, especially students who will return to China with knowledge gained from the higher education provided by the United States.

8. Fentanyl drugs are killing over 100,000 of our youth each year, supplied by Chinese and Mexican organized cartels. Despite threats and gestures

from Trump to China, waving our fists has not stopped these toxic imports. Although a recent agreement on Chinese cooperation has emerged, will China follow through on these promises, or will it ignore them as in the past?

There are likely many other areas where China conflicts with the United States, such as space dominance, AI leadership (a significant concern), and possibly replacing the dollar with a Super Yen as a key part of global trade. There are probably other unnamed areas aimed at securing Chinese dominance.

I am confident that President Trump is aware of the increasing strategic competition between the U.S. and China, so far without nuclear weapons or invasions. However, he prefers not to alarm Americans or the world by openly declaring war. Instead, he is using tariffs to gradually reduce our reliance on China and on imports, which will not only level the playing field but also likely worsen China's deep economic issues. These implied tariffs on China and Asia will eventually promote the formation of new businesses and manufacturing, as well as the transfer of key raw materials to the United States and its allies. But what actions will China take?

In 2025, the imbalance between our exports and imports with China (1:4) is helping fund China's military and other activities, which may not align with U.S. strategic priorities. For many reasons, we must put an end to this.

Potential Problems

Lord Jason Stockwood recently said, "AI isn't a substitute for specific human jobs but rather a general labor substitute for humans. Massive headcount reductions are already underway in the technology industry. We are going to have to think carefully about how we soft land those industries that go away, with some form of universal relief and a lifelong learning mechanism as well, so people can retrain."

Stockwood has previously proposed taxing tech companies to fund a universal basic income.

Corporate management will have to consider mechanisms to absorb a large temporary displacement that will cut deeply for several years.

One solution is to have humanoid robots provide full-time, in-depth instruction to upskill laid-off workers and help them meet new job eligibility requirements. This could easily be paired with a special tax on companies that use ten or more robots.

Summary

The problem with writing a book about current policy or events is that, unlike in the past, the horizon is not 20/20. Events unforeseen for the most part, as a writer looks to the future, only to find that his assumptions are far different from those forecasted. As you consider the variables ahead of us, we cannot accurately calculate the prospects of war, the role of our financial system, or our leaders' reactions to the changing events that will undoubtedly present themselves, particularly over the next three to four years.

I'm reminded of the Ombudsman hired years ago by The New York Times to determine how deeply left-wing writing had crept into the newspaper's various departments, if at all. It was painful to learn that the Ombudsman found liberal bias in nearly every section of the newspaper, even the Book Review. I'm not sure what they did about sports, but we were well before the flag-burning and BLM that sometimes erupts with our professional sports teams.

To give credit where it's due, the New York Times did publish a study showing that its bias was pervasive across the paper's departments.

Instead of an affront, they probably read this with pride and mild interest, then proceeded to tailor their efforts to the growing use of LIE-WARE to savage their political enemies and get Democrats to toe the party line.

I really do not think there'll ever be a system that will rein in stretching the truth or political editing. It is too tempting, too fun, too profitable, and too useful for their purposes. Frankly, I include all mass media, social media, and blogs, as well as both parties, in this statement.

All we can do is cite examples from the past and claim they were joyous, not only for politicians but also for their readers, listeners, and viewers. The moroseness Democrats currently feel is entirely preventable, but I can't think of any basic cure for the continual knocking of America and its progress in '24, or for plans to improve. If the Democrats had won, I'm sure the Republicans would also be in a morose decline about politics; however, in general, I think the conservatives are more upbeat, spiritual, and happy campers who will soldier on. I also believe the Democrats will soldier on. My only hope is that they become aware of and circumspect about the fake news they are being fed, and, more often than not, seek out the other point of view to provide balance in their thinking. I think America is strong and enduring. We have a sound political system that works. I think the two-party system keeps the other party honest and responsible, so I have every hope for the country's future.

As we navigate tomorrow's complex technologies, confront the enormity of many foreign policy concerns, and address issues such as immigration, the Fed, the economy, and public safety, we must keep our eyes wide open and our hands on the real data to proceed.

Considering the political implications that brought us here in the first place, I think we will smooth out the rough edges of progress. And those of us who will live much longer into the Century will begin to glimpse that "Shining Citadel on the Hill," our destiny unless we succumb to the noise.

Author's Note

When I began writing this book, I vowed not to be one-sided but to be even-handed in my treatment of our two major political parties. I've tried, but the more I've gotten into it, the more I realize this democracy has enemies not only in Asia and the Mideast, but also here at home. Frankly, Democrats recently have tried to block everything positive that Republicans have tried to do, particularly since the 2024 election. The Democratic Party has long been the party of the people. They have brought the American people Women's Suffrage, plus Social Security and Medicare/Medicaid, providing a safety net for all retiring Americans. After World War II, they educated our military with the G.I. Bill. These have been tremendous contributions to American society. However, in recent years, particularly since Trump's first election, they have come out primarily with negativity, TDS, and a barrier to progress in this country. They have maliciously closed the government for political purposes and fought, for example, against the "Big, Beautiful Bill," which will provide tremendous cuts for all tax-paying Americans in 2026 and beyond.

For the past hundred years, the left-leaning media has dominated most of the media, including TV, radio, newspapers, magazines, and, more recently, social media. Recently, this percentage has declined to a whopping seventy percent (my estimate) as Fox properties have made inroads with a more conservative approach. The problem with a dominant media is that the public has little chance to see any other side of the news beyond what is crafted by liberals. I believe this will change in 2026-28 and beyond. Meanwhile, we have seventy million people who, over many years, have been indoctrinated into the party that was the party of the people, which now appears to be embracing socio-communism in its major cities. Hopefully, this will change in the future, as we desperately need a valid two-party system that provides checks and balances as we push forward toward a beautiful, golden future. Today, with AI, vast investments in technology and business, and with hard work and prudence, our future generations will come to see that shining city on the hill that gave promise to so many of our "struggling masses yearning to be free."

Thank you for reading Lie-Ware
--Raleigh Coffin
2026

LIE-WARE QUESTIONNAIRE

Do you think opening our borders has benefited the United States?

Was reducing our energy use by 30% on the first day of the Biden administration a good move for our economy and for our foreign policy?

Do you believe that socialism, which has never succeeded anywhere, should be an option for the Democratic Party?

Do you believe we should allow Iran to develop nuclear capabilities?

Do you believe the FED has been fair in its rate decisions?

Do you believe that Biden was not influenced by outside sources and took responsibility for the country throughout his term?

Do you think the Green Lobby had accurate weather data to predict severe global warming?

Did you think that E-cars should have had a purchase incentive compared with standard autos?

Do you think the Big Beautiful Bill, which cut taxes by 58%, was a good decision?

Do you think the wealthiest 2.2% of individuals should pay more than the total income tax they currently owe?

Do you believe that tariffs are inflationary and hurt our economy rather than benefit it?

Do you think the lawlessness in sanctuary cities should be upheld and supported by the US?

Do you believe that defunding the police is a good policy for a city or a state?

Do you think allowing "trans-men" to compete in women's events is fair from a physics or legitimacy standpoint?

Do you believe Donald Trump should be prosecuted for his actions in Iran and Venezuela?

Would you vote for a Socio-Communist leader for your city-state or country, like in New York City?

Are you supporting Hamas or Israel in their struggle for dominance?

Are you in favor of or against ICE's policies?

Raileigh Coffin, President of CBS/Fox International,
Circa 1990

www.ingramcontent.com/pod-product-compliance
Lightning Source LLC
LaVergne TN
LVHW010921110826
845155LV00037B/428

9781970153590